Collection of life stories
of the survivors
of the Quebec Indian Residential Schools

Coordination: Richard Gray and Martine Gros-Louis Monier

Writing: Les ateliers du Maître

Conduction of interviews: AS Média

Translation: Wendatraduction

Revision: Richard Gray

Design and illustrations: Christiane Vincent

Printing: Les Copies de la Capitale Inc.

This document was produced by the:

First Nations of Quebec and Labrador Health and Social Services Commission

250 place Chef Michel Laveau, Suite 102

Wendake (Quebec) G0A 4V0

Phone: 418-842-1540

Fax: 418-842-7045

Website: www.cssspnql.com

This document is available in French.

March 2010

ISBN: 978-1-926553-30-6

Introduction

Since ancient times, the First Nations have inhabited the Earth. They have travelled across it, taken from it the necessities of life and joy, and derived knowledge and wisdom from it. They have always learned through observation. Therefore speech, when it occurs, targets the essential elements: the lost trail, an attack or a message from the Creator.

It is therefore in a context of profound silence that the First Nations have dealt with a level of distress so profound that in order to put an end to it, they nearly lost themselves.

First of all, the communities were relocated, isolated and placed within restricted territories – they were impoverished. Then, the family connections were severed. The children were isolated and placed in territories that were devoid of joy, love and meaning. These types of places attack the soul, impede growth and prevent loving and being loved. How do you rebuild a life that has been destroyed?

The time has come for words that are necessary and just. Then, an entire story was told, the story of the First Nations of Canada and the senseless acts that they were subjected to, day after day, simply to take away their lands, their languages, their culture - so that they would be no more.

There was an increasing number of voices talking about the irreparable losses. Sometimes, the voices were just whispers - sometimes they were weeping and other times resentful. Nonetheless, the voices are very real and what they are saying is the truth. Everyone who hears the voices is concerned because the story is both terrible and true.

Today, these voices are reforming the unravelled connections. They are saying "Don't remain alone; come along. Remember who we are, remember our artistry, our worldly knowledge, and the language of our Forefathers. We cannot, nor do we wish to, turn back time. However, we must stop living in fear and shame. Remember who you are."

In these times during which the world is changing, the need for speaking out has come, as has the time for guides, the time for those who were lost and have returned to the trail, who once again are listening to the language of their Forefathers. These are the people you will hear from here. They are normal human beings who have suffered; people who have been roaming around and forgetting themselves after having experienced countless losses. Yet today, their voices once again include laughter, love, pride and hope.

The circle says that nothing is definitive – everything that befalls eventually passes and then something else happens. The circle says that nobody can live and survive alone, that everything is absolutely interconnected and what we leave behind inevitably changes a little later, further down the road. Therefore, us the First Nations, us the First Peoples, let's observe, listen and come together.

Table of contents

Photo: Patrice Gosselin

"There are days when my anger is less intense. I have provided myself with tools. When I feel my anger coming, I play the guitar. I listen to my guitar and when it sounds aggressive, I know that it's my anger. I can feel it. And when it sounds melodious, I know that I'm at peace with myself."

Alex
Lac Simon, St Marc de Figuery

I was born in Rapid Seven. That was the land of my parents. My father passed away when I was five years old. I barely remember him, which did not help me at all when I entered the Indian residential school.

In Rapid Seven, we lived in cabins, in the forest, with my mother's family. Before my father passed away, he was a wood cutter and a logger. I remember that I would visit him at his work. He died from a common accident – in a moment of carelessness, he fell into the water and drowned. It was the fall season and because of the clothing he wore, he sank quickly. That is all I know about the story of his passing.

When I entered the residential school, I was six-and-a-half years old. I remember them telling my brother John and me to get into the car. Once we got to the residential school, it was as if we became strangers. It was like a separation, he did his own things and we each had our own group of friends. He was in a rival gang. It was different with William, my youngest brother. When I got into the residential school, I was so lost. He was also lost and I remember how I felt when I got close to him, and so I tried to get near him as often as possible.

When I entered the residential school, it was a completely different world. I didn't even know what a shower was. A light with a switch was foreign to me – strange and bizarre – and I didn't know a word of French. The only thing I could say in French was "My name is Alex." It was my mother who had taught me how to say that. I also knew the word bread, "some bread". When I received instructions, I couldn't understand anything and so they would hit me. It became brutal. The first night and my first shower had a big effect on me. When I felt the water jets on my body, I really enjoyed the feeling. But the monitor who was there had a squeegee of sorts that served to remove water from the bottom of the tub. He pulled me really hard with it from behind my head and I slipped and fell. I think I broke my nose. Ever since that time I have had problems breathing. I'm not sure if that was the cause, but I think it was.

The first two years were very difficult. I was having problems with the French language. From the very first days at school, everything was so brutal. Since I was left-handed, they would hit me with a ruler because they wanted me to write with my right hand. I was always on the lookout because eventually I understood that they were upset with me because I was writing with my left hand. Therefore, I would pretend to write with my right hand and then I would switch hands when the brother wasn't looking. He ended up understanding that he was wasting his time. As for me, once I could finally understand French, I understood that the left hand was considered to be the hand of the devil. And so, in my childhood mind, I believed that I was the devil. This was both disturbing and really bothersome to me. As time passed, because of the rules, I became a child who was always confrontational – I was a defiant child. I am still that way today – only not as bad as before.

We are like onions; today I see my life one layer at a time. Sometimes, smells, sounds or music remind me of those times, which were sometimes sad and sometimes happy. I didn't feel sad for the entire four years that I was there. When you're a little boy, you learn to adapt - you find a way to have fun regardless of what's going on. At the residential school, if it wasn't for hockey, I would have gone crazy. Sport became my support. Until I was thirty years old, I played and when I was on the ice, I would let it all out. As soon as I saw an opponent, I would do my best to body check him as hard as I could. Perhaps that was one of the reasons why I hung up my skates early.

At the residential school there was physical, psychological and even sexual abuse. That was what I was subjected to. That was the hardest thing to talk about, to express.

When life returned to its normal course, I didn't have any points of reference. I only had my mother who was a very authoritative person. She couldn't speak French. She tried to get me to understand that I was the oldest and therefore had certain responsibilities. So, she exercised her authority in the Algonquin language and we didn't have a choice but to listen. The Anishnabe. She was always after us to ensure that we learned the language and she talked to me about being responsible and the example I was giving as the eldest child.

In the 1960s and 70s, the government allowed Indians a little more breathing room. There was a provincial school here in Louvicourt and so I went to that school before going to the high school in Alma.

When I got out of the residential school, I was living in a state of anger. But I was unable to identify the source of the anger, since it was buried so deep within me. Because of the omnipresent religion at the residential school, we were not allowed to express our emotions, especially anger, because they said it would cause us to burn in hell for eternity. Once I began to understand French, I thought that eternity seemed like an awfully long time to burn in hell for. I remember having trouble sleeping whenever I made an error or a mistake, since I was afraid of burning in hell. In my childhood mind, it was terrifying. It still bothered me until I turned thirty years old.

As a child, I learned how to numb my emotions in order to avoid feeling anything. When my father passed away, I remember comforting my mother; I believed that I was in control, but in reality I wasn't really living, I was just numb. Eventually, it was my addictions that did the work. Today, I am starting to feel happy, to feel well, my emotions aren't as intense. I still feel them but knowing where they come from is a source of relief.

I started using at a very young age, at around fourteen years old. Using was my crutch for a while, a terrible crutch, but a means of escape. Fortunately, I was really into sports. We would train and were disciplined – but after the hockey games, we would celebrate our victories. Eventually I was even drinking because I had lost, and then at one point I no longer knew why I was drinking. I had created my own hell.

I got married when I was fairly young. We had three daughters. My eldest daughter was often sad. It was my behaviour that made her feel that way. One morning, I brought my entire family to Domrémy. It marked the first time that I sought help. I saw other people who had succeeded in putting an end to their addictions and they seemed to be doing well. I also wanted to feel well. I went to a few AA meetings. I was at war with religion so as soon as they recited the Our Father, I left. I returned one-and-a-half years later. I learned that it was just a prayer. I started sorting myself out as well; I learned that religion and spirituality were two different things. I started making distinctions. I learned that with respect to those who had abused me - it was not religion that was the cause but rather individuals. I started making sense of all these different things.

Collection of life stories of the survivors of the Quebec Indian Residential Schools

The thing that helped me progress was my return to school in 1996. I resumed my studies to obtain a bachelor's degree in social work in Val d'Or. During the first year, three times per week, I hitchhiked in minus thirty weather dressed like an astronaut. As a young adult that had always been my goal – I wanted to become a social worker. It took me four years. There were times when I needed to come to grips with what had happened to me, to look back on my past and the burden that continued to follow me around. I still didn't realize the place the residential school had in my life. I was trying to escape it. My studies also enabled me to quit using alcohol and drugs for four years. I was able to see the difference. However, once per year I gave myself permission to celebrate. Oftentimes, I had the feeling that I was going crazy, especially near the end of the semesters when projects had to be handed in.

When I graduated, I worked with men in my area facilitating social reintegration in detention centres as a probation officer. This lasted for a year and a half. The suicide attempt signs had started appearing. There was a week in which we dealt with three suicide attempts. That was when I started having nightmares. I was seeing bodies everywhere. I had a stroke one year after the suicide attempts had begun. I had gone into the forest for fasting purposes, and when I returned I hadn't followed the rules. I pushed myself much too hard and suffered a stroke. After that, I changed my life. I didn't just clean things up, I simply changed lives and then I made adjustments. When I returned to work, I said "end of contract." Then I left Lac Simon.

My wife and I separated and then a position opened up in Val d'Or. I performed the needs assessments that needed to be carried out in order to help the youth. One day, the high school principal said to me, "I don't think it's normal that in a school, half the students that arrive from elementary school require special classes. I don't understand all these learning disorders we're seeing. " I therefore started reading up on learning disorders. I met with a professor from the *Université de Sherbrooke* who had performed a study in a community on learning disorders. I followed that path and it lead me back to the Indian residential schools. I obtained documentation from the Aboriginal Healing Foundation. I started seeking information – I wanted to know who these children were and who their parents were. They were the second and third generations, and all of the problems originated from the residential schools. At the school, I became upset with the non-Aboriginal teachers. It was no longer working out and so I handed in my resignation. The root of the problem was the rage that I kept inside that I was unable to eliminate.

I was still in the process of progressing and, in 1995, I came in contact with Aboriginal spirituality. I met the person who remained my mentor until he passed away in 2003. He came from Maniwaki. He took me under his wing and when he passed away, like Jesus and the apostles, I had been following him blindly. It was very difficult for me to get back on track. Our mother passed away that winter.

At the hearing, in the month of May, I underwent a psychological evaluation that had a profound impact on me. When I got out, I had the feeling that my spirit was walking beside me. I was exhausted. I understood then why they covered two nights in a hotel.

And then, I had really strange dreams.

In the first dream, I arrive beside a lake. I see children who are playing on the shore, but they don't see me. I am an adult. I approach the children who are holding hands and going around in circles. There are children of different colours: brown, yellow and black. As I move towards the lake, garbage bags start coming out of the water. Garbage – lots of garbage, and it's pouring out of the water. I turn around and I see garbage everywhere. I move towards the children and then one of them smiles at me. I go and play with them, and go round and round in circles with them.

Shortly afterwards, on the same night, I had another strange dream. I am in my room and I dream of the room that I'm sleeping in. There are broken chairs and many other broken objects and I don't want to change anything. The floor waiter comes to take everything away but I don't let him. I get angry with the man. Eventually, I decide to let go and when they are finished picking everything up, they bring me a nice dish, a good meal - something really delicious.

Of course, I interpreted these dreams. In the first dream, the water represents emotions. The fact that there are children means that the emotions have been there for a long time. I was seeing myself like a child in an adult's body. Finally, the child cleans everything up. I am the only adult in this dream.

In the second dream, I see the need to let go, which is what I did later on. There were old things that I was holding on to and I ended up throwing everything out – even the old pair of pants. I cleaned out my closet.

My biggest dream is one that I dream while I'm awake. I want to help others, go into the forest, build a cabin and return to my roots. I worked a lot with elders and therefore learned much about culture and spirituality. I would simply like to live in the forest; I know that I would survive, even in the winter when it's most difficult.

What I would really like is for people to start opening their eyes. People aren't talking to each other, they are shutting themselves away. Pettiness is rampant, as is gossiping. The people underestimate themselves and they underestimate others as well. People should start appreciating themselves and others too.

For me, being a First Nations person means being part of a people that some tried to exterminate. We are just trying to be who we were and who we wanted to be. And it isn't over, this is just the beginning. Some are still asleep, but others are now awake.

In life we ask ourselves who we are. When we are unable to answer that question, we cry. I didn't know who I was, and I thought about it a lot. I did everything for others to avoid losing my friends. What was difficult was that everything that made me who I was as a person wasn't considered important. That was what the residential schools had taught us – what the Catholic religion had taught us. It was a source of internal conflict, a general conflict that affected my values and ways of doing things. Just talking about oneself was considered selfish. Sometimes it felt like a dream to discuss what I had experienced. At the hearing, I was in a state of emotional shock. It was afterwards that the facts came back to me clearly.

I have not yet reached the stage of forgiveness and reconciliation. It's very difficult for me to accept the way things are and the things that have happened. In order to reconcile, I need to be able to accept what I went through and I haven't made it that far yet. There are days when my anger is less intense. I have provided myself with tools. When I feel my anger coming, I play the guitar. I listen to my guitar and when it sounds aggressive, I know that it's my anger. I can feel it. And when it sounds melodious, I know that I'm at peace with myself. In the wintertime, I vent by shovelling snow. I split wood. Sometimes people offer their help and I turn them down by saying, "No, it's alright, I'll do it on my own". It helps me; it's a release. "You should open a window to toss the wood in", "No, no", I reply. I want to take my time bringing in the wood and taking it downstairs. Doing this helps me to live in the present. I want to really live in the present, because if I don't, what's the use? In the past I was unable to do this. I want to relieve my burden - particularly the things are the most cumbersome. It's always been a process for me.

Helping others served as a lifeline for me for a long time. I learned that I had to take care of myself as well with things that are important to me: guitar, arts, giving shows, wood, spirituality and sweat lodges. Now I am doing well. Today, music helps me a lot. It allows me to express myself.

My hearing took place on May 16th; when I found out the date, I panicked. I couldn't take the time to live anymore, I wasn't sleeping anymore, and I always had to be doing something to stay busy. I am currently performing research on suicide prevention. My children have always known that I went to a residential school. They were also subjected to the effects of the residential school. Our children are also getting older. The first time, it was very difficult for me to answer their questions. Today, when I answer them, it's always quite a story and they are always quite happy to listen to me. I have met residential school survivors and young parents who know nothing about the history of the residential schools. I facilitated a project among young adults who knew nothing about the residential schools and it marked the first time that I had a young person ask me "What are residential schools?"; it was strange because I knew this person's parents well; both of them went to a residential school but they had never discussed the matter with their child. The young person had just learned something important and was very confused.

Photo: Patrice Gosselin

"We were so uncommunicative. I had never made the connection with the residential schools. It is still hard for me. I believed my behaviour was normal because there were many of us in the community who were former residential school students and we all acted the same way."

Anne-Marie
Matimekush-Lac John

My name is Anne-Marie and I come from Matimekush-Lac John. I went to the Maliotenam residential school. I've completely erased it from my mind. I don't even remember how I got there anymore. And I left when it closed in 1972. I was in grade 2 when I arrived at the residential school. My brother, sister, uncles and aunts were there as well. We all went to the residential school. I was raised by my grandparents, because my mother left me.

Before the residential school, I was always in the forest. My fondest memories are from time spent in the woods. We would leave in the month of August after the Virgin Mary procession. Fishing was what interested me the most. When the residential school closed, I returned to the community.

Sometimes at the residential school, on weekends, they took us into the forest and we would go for a walk. I really enjoyed that. As time passed we made friends – we went sliding and skating. When I left the residential school, I started high school. I returned to the school here. All of these events left a profound impact on us but we didn't talk about it. In order to heal, I would go into the forest. My relationship with my grandparents hasn't changed. My grandmother was the one who showed me everything and educated me. I listened to her and that was what helped me the most. She passed away at ninety-three years of age. I had two children. They were also a source of healing for me.

At around eighteen or nineteen years of age, I started having addictions issues. I started thinking about dealing with my addictions because I worked for the band council and I heard people talking about healing projects. I went through the process and received compensation. Then, we benefitted from projects. We went into the forest with two psychologists. For the first two days, nobody wanted to talk about it. It took some time. We also did other activities. The group expanded – there were some new members. We were so uncommunicative. I had never made the connection with the residential schools. It is still hard for me. I believed my behaviour was normal because there were many of us in the community who were former residential school students and we all acted the same way. One of my cousins wanted to come with us to the residential school. She was disappointed that she couldn't come, because they only sent the children whose parents went into the forest. Many still have a hard time talking about what happened.

I used both drugs and alcohol. I stopped when I noticed that I was no longer able to function properly. What helped me the most to stop using were the meetings in the forest. They were held once per week. When I was there I could reconnect with the experiences I had when I was young and with my grandparents. After the years I spent at the residential school, whenever my grandfather would drop a net into the lake in the winter, I was the one who went with him. I would hurry before the guys asked to go with him. That was before I got married. After I got married, I returned to Schefferville. We lived in the forest for three months and that is a beautiful memory for my children. My daughter didn't like going into the forest but my son really enjoyed it.

I have five grandchildren, one of whom lives with us. He is two years old. I would like to pass on to my grandchildren a love for nature, just like my grandmother once did for me. She would always take me with her. We would get up early in the morning. The guys would see to the traps. We always went to the same spot. There was a small log cabin that my grandfather built with a woodstove inside. My grandmother would clean the furs and I wanted to help her. She removed the meat from the fur. She was worried that I would damage her marten, mink, fox and wolf skins. My grandparents sold fur. I watched her and learned what to do but she didn't want me to help her. She also set up snares around the cabin. One day, she and I had a duck cooking contest, but there was no winner.

I always spoke my language with my grandparents. When we returned here, my children spoke only French. They learned the Innu language while playing with the other children. It's my grandchildren who bring me joy today. I am very proud to be a First Nations person. My hope is that my children will reconnect with the culture of our people as well as our traditional values. I don't know why things change so much. Television is changing everything. Here, once per year, everything closes during cultural week: the school, the band council and so on and so forth, and then everyone goes into the forest. The youth really enjoy it. It takes place in the month of May during goose-hunting season. We get ready, set up camp and then everyone goes hunting. My job is to pluck the feathers from the geese.

Sometimes I go snowshoeing alone in the forest if there is still snow. I enjoy it. I've always enjoyed wandering off into the forest on my own.

I'm Catholic but I don't pray very often - only when I need to. I practiced Lent in order to pray a little more. I didn't experience any changes in my religion as a result of the residential school. I was more upset with my mother who wasn't there for me. She left me and I never knew my father. My mother has now returned. Today, she is seventy-six years old and we take care of her.

I was more of a mother for my children. I was very close to them. My son has four children and we are still very close today. My grandfather cried when I got married. My husband is a Malecite and I've had a happy life with him. I re-established a family but my children weren't raised in the forest.

Photo: Patrice Gosselin

"Everyday life was a process of teaching and learning without anybody telling us that we were worthless. We lived simply while working on many daily chores; we knew how to live on our own. It was happiness and I know many stories of happy childhoods."

Catherine

Micmac, Shubnagidy Residential School.

My life before the residential school was very peaceful. I believe that the memories of my childhood have maintained my Aboriginal identify despite the residential school, thanks to my Creator-given ability to forget those difficult years. For forty to fifty years, I had forgotten my life at the residential school. I remembered in the 1990s and then I started having problems. I had to deal with everything I had experienced. I had to learn to manage the pain and anger I had inside me because of everything I was subjected to in addition to sexual abuse. I started having nightmares. I was barely sleeping and crying a lot. I wasn't sleeping in the same bed as my husband. I couldn't function anymore. I went through a severe depression and I am still in therapy. I see doctors and I take medication. As of right now, I feel as though I'll probably never get through it. Others are able to get past it – I see those people, so I know.

When the RCMP came, we were gathering wood for the winter. We were together and we were well. I was eight years old. Somebody ran up to us and said "The police are here, your father wants you to go in the house." We thought something had happened to my mother. At home, my mother was crying and my father went outside. We were put into in a vehicle and taken away. On our way, we picked up other children, here and there, from other reserves in the area. They brought us to the train station without luggage, with only what we were wearing. The children were crying and asking where their parents were. We travelled by train all day long. In the evening, we arrived at the residential school. Nuns made us get off the train. They lined us up, two by two, in the dark. The children were crying. Upon our arrival at the residential school, they cut our hair and undressed us so they could wash us. They hit us and told us to be quiet, to stop crying. It's hard for me to think about, it distresses me. They treated us like a bunch of savages.

That was how we started school. I probably spent four years at the residential school. I saw a lot of unfortunate things. We had no rights: we didn't have the right to be too happy, or the right to laugh, or the right to cry, or the right to sing, or the right to speak our language. This caused us to shut ourselves off to the world. We couldn't express our emotions. Whenever people came to visit us, they would ask us to smile.

At the residential school, I worked in the kitchen. I started my day at four in the morning in order to make breakfast for the entire school – nuns and priests included. Afterwards, I went to class for an hour or two. Then, I made lunch and dinner and I did this every day. Starting in the third year, everyone had chores; for the first two years, we didn't have any. We didn't spend much time in the classroom, only three to four hours per day. They would tell us how worthless we were. I remember that much more than the lessons.

I didn't know that my problems came from the residential school. I had kept everything bottled up inside. For fifty or sixty years, we pretended that it had never happened. When I met people who went to the residential school, we didn't talk about it, we never did. No survivor ever discussed the residential school with me. The Micmac Nation lived in darkness, because nobody wanted to talk about those sad years. Nobody wanted to remember them. Even I, as someone who went to a residential school, didn't know that the generations before me had attended as well. I only learned this in the 1990s.

I could recognize those who attended residential schools. I could see the impact that it had on them and on their families. There are parents who don't know how to love, how to show affection. There are some families of survivors who treat their children the way they were treated at school. For example, they all take their baths together with their underwear on. That's how they wash their children. It's a sad story that will last for as long as there are survivors. It doesn't matter if we tell our children that it is now part of the past.

Aboriginal people were not allowed to exist as Aboriginal people. They took from us the moral values that came with the language: respect, human dignity, love for children and the heritage of this love, unity. I could talk for a long time about everything we have lost. I am telling my story so that people can start to understand, and also so that I can succeed in forgiving humanity - the same humanity that couldn't accept that Aboriginals were human-beings with a different culture. It's hard to think about the future of my people. The major impact, for me, is that I'm unable to move forward. For a long time in my life, I was a creative person. I would organize, direct and work for others.

Then suddenly, I couldn't do anything anymore. I am here to share my story with you and it's the only thing I'm able to do.

I am very stubborn; I don't get discouraged very easily. I didn't forget my language even if at the residential school they prevented me from speaking it. If a nun or priest caught me speaking my language, they pulled my hair and humiliated me. That didn't keep me from thinking in my language. So long as I can think and keep the language in my mind, I want to continue and I will continue. My hope is for my family, for Aboriginal people and for all of humanity to get out of this dead end and see all of the beautiful things we could achieve together. That is what motivates me.

For me, a happy childhood is berry-picking, swimming, climbing trees, helping an elderly lady braid her hair, helping her to wash, spending time with my mother and father, watching my father sculpt birds and animals with his knife and helping my mother make baskets. The mothers letting the children add the finishing touches to the baskets. Everyday life was a process of teaching and learning without anybody telling us that we were worthless. We lived simply while working on many daily chores; we knew how to live on our own. It was happiness and I know many stories of happy childhoods.

That's what encourages me to go on. I remember being on a small boat with my father; I learned while helping him, without being beaten or humiliated.

Being Aboriginal, does it have to have a meaning? For me, it means that I'm alive, that the Creator recognizes me, that I live on the earth and that I have a right to be on this planet. I live my life the way I choose to. I do not deviate from my path. I don't wear any feathers and I don't have to. I once went to a museum with other Aboriginal people. We spoke in our language, our Micmac language. A stranger asked me where my feathers were. I told him I was an Aboriginal person, not a bird. I don't have to try to be like others. I like to be different, in fact I love it. I love being alive and I really want to heal from the effects of the residential school experience, because it caused a lot of harm in my life, to my family and to my people. I want peace and love for all of the communities.

Some nations have ceased speaking their language and others have ceased to evolve. We have developed an individualistic and materialistic mentality rather than pursuing our tradition of taking care of each other. All of humanity, not only us but particularly us, was affected because of the way we lived. The influence of the residential school system and the war and soldier era had an impact on us. Now, it's television. It's no longer even reality that is influencing us, but a false reality.

For my children as well as the next seven generations, I ask that they live in harmony and be at peace with themselves. I wish everyone inner spirituality. I try to teach my children, to teach them with wisdom. I have educated and learned children. I tell them "Remember who you are and learn with wisdom, because these things can be passed on. Stupidity is everywhere but wisdom is not." My role as a grandmother today is difficult to describe, because my grandchildren live far away and everywhere. We talk but it's not the same. I only see them twice per year; we are losing a lot of time. I cannot fully contribute because I'm only there in passing.

I don't know if we will be able to return to the life we once lived, a life that can return our Aboriginal identity to us. Nowadays, we leave others to do things on our behalf and decide for us instead of taking control of ourselves. We are isolating ourselves from a functional society and we are not constructive for this reason. We aren't contributing. It will take us a long time to find our mentality. We must break out of our isolation and dissention; we have a lot of work ahead of us.

We are fighting in a corporate world – even the governments are struggling with corporations that are hungry and ready to do anything. Nestle is an example of such a company: it sets up in a country and dries up the land by draining all the water. How do we stop these people? All of the fertile lands that are needed for humanity's survival are being used up by large corporations. When I look around, I see less water, soil and trees that hold the soil in place and more and more tree cutting, landslides and ecological impacts that the rich believe we can't see. We have lived here for thousands of years. It must be repeated – the corporations must be accountable.

Before, our governance was based on treaties. Our government was the Grand Council. We had a single Chief for all of the Micmac people and he was in charge of the Nations of the Atlantic, Maine and New England. Everyone agreed with this situation. Everything was disrupted when the English arrived. The Micmac people lived for one hundred years with the French before their expulsion and they got along well. When we returned from the residential schools, we were no longer accepted. We were banished and rejected; we were no longer welcome. Many couldn't speak our language anymore. The Elders couldn't understand us anymore while 90% of us left for the United States or elsewhere. When Aboriginal people received the right to vote, they were also allowed to go to the bank and purchase alcohol - quite a gift indeed.

"I am playing in the light breeze,

The weather is nice,

My mother is here, my father isn't far away,

I feel safe and protected.

Then one day, they take me away,

My mother can't hide her fear and my father has lost his spirit."

Before, I used to sing. Today, I don't sing anymore. I lost my voice - I lost my singing soul.

"All those years it was my mother that I had been looking for, for her love; when I finally understood that, I was then able to see my partner as a man and love him as my spouse — as a human-being."

Denise

My name is Denise Coocoo – and I spent seven years at the Pointe Bleue residential school.

My spouse and I, we speak to each other, we call each other "my love" and we are like children pretending to be adults. He often says to me, "It's because we didn't have a childhood and so we are living it today." I reply that it isn't the same thing, that all that joy, playing with one's parents, laughing, running - today it's as if I really don't have the capacity for these types of things. I'm fifty years old; I cannot play as if I were a child. I accompany people into hearings and I understand when we are told that it is never too late to live one's childhood. But when I listen to the survivor express what he/she feels, I also understand when he/she explains that it's not the same living one's childhood at fifty years of age as when you can live it at four or five years of age. I am realistic today and I am able to tell myself that I had a sad childhood, and that I experienced pain; I'm able to accept it. What I experienced, saw and heard makes me the person that I am. I would not have had this son or these grandchildren. I went through a difficult relationship for ten years and it's because of this relationship that I had my son. I don't have any regrets.

When I got out of the residential schools, I didn't really think that there could be things that needed changing, I didn't even have the ability to think nor did I have any skills. I had only learned to do what I saw or what I was told to do. I was five years old when I left. Today, I know that right from the start I was broken, everything that I was before had been damaged. Over the years, this sentiment was reinforced by repetitive departures. It was caused by being taken away - the rupture, the separation with my parents. In my childhood memories, I never cried, I had the same two or three images in my mind for years. I saw a little girl in a bus that I knew was me and she wasn't crying or saying anything. In another image, I see myself lying in a bed staring at the ceiling, repeating to myself, "I'm at home, I'm at home, I'm…" When I woke up and opened my eyes at the residential school, my childhood heart was broken.

After a few years, I didn't feel good when I was at home either. I wasn't aware of it but the anger that I was carrying around with me kept building up to the point where I wasn't comfortable anywhere. Afterwards, when I got out of the residential school, the departures continued to happen. I had to go into town into a foster family. Without any control, things were very different. They provided an amount of money to go shopping for clothing. We were four in this foster family and we didn't even know how to make decisions regarding our clothing. We all bought ourselves the same things; we dressed identically, just like we learned at the residential school. When we walked on sidewalks we walked two-by-two, in a double file. We had no sense of individuality. At the residential school, we didn't need to decide anything, there was no need for thinking – we were given everything – even toothpaste, soap, etc.

Without this control, without the threat from the police, our parents or prison, it became so easy to run away. I started using both drugs and alcohol when I was fifteen years old and I kept having addictions issues for years and years and years. I married a former residential school student and we had a difficult relationship for ten years. The first time I made the decision to leave was when I left ten years later. My son was seven years old and he came with me – he was the one who decided to come with me. I wasn't in a state in which I would be able to care for him.

My addictions were controlling me and it was my son who woke me up. When I used alcohol or drugs, I would say to him, "I'll buy you this" or "I'll buy you that", but then he started yelling at me, "It's not true! You're lying to me mom!" Even though I'm crying as I tell my story, it's still much easier to tell it than it once was. Each time I talk about it, each time I tell my story, I get better and better. Under normal circumstances, I am well with myself, I have a new peace of mind, and I no longer feel bad like I once did. When I get involved in various healing activities, it helps me to see where it still hurts, where it's sensitive, where there is still work to be done. Only time can heal certain wounds. When I managed to overcome my depression and once I pulled through, everything changed.

When I left my son's father, I also left the community. My son always wanted to go back and yet he never did – I didn't know why. His father informed me that when he went back, the other children would say to him "Your mother isn't here because she left your dad." He was sick and tired of hearing it. It was always my son who woke me up or made me aware of my situation; he made me see, through his experience, the type of mother I was and what I was teaching him.

When I decided to put an end to my addictions, since I was the one who made that decision, I didn't get any help, I did it on my own, and after three years, I started again and I hit rock bottom again.

My ex-husband advised me to call the health centre to tell them that I had an addictions problem. I called, but I didn't really believe that I had a problem. I told them what I was told to tell them. They referred me to detoxification treatment. After twenty-one days of treatment, normally they keep you for twenty-one days, I was only starting to feel better. I didn't want to leave. I felt alone. I was afraid to get out and end up outside. I received detoxification services for thirty-three days.

My fear was to face a world that I didn't know. I felt afraid, destitute. It marked the first time I really felt what was living inside of me. I was functioning in a daze while following others. Doing as others did was reassuring to me and it eventually turned into an addiction. I relapsed often. I could stop for five years – and then relapse again. I tried AA, I asked questions. I would talk about my addictions but I never discussed the residential schools. When I participated in AA meetings, I didn't feel well. I had stopped drinking but things weren't going well at all. I was full of fear and anger.

I did the most work on myself in 2006. I had achieved what I was looking for, what I had always wanted. While working on certain projects, I saw the repercussions of the residential schools at all levels in the population: the fear, the worry, the lack of care for others, speaking against others - not because we were evil, but rather because that's what the residential schools had turned us into. I also suffered from these repercussions and I had to be in front of the others while knowing that it was preventing me from doing a good job and having good values such as respect, kindness and sharing. The repercussions were preventing me from being who I wanted to be. I knew that I had to change.

I was born in 1959 and the first time I heard someone talking about residential schools was at a gathering in Trois-Rivières in 1999. After it was over, I went into my room crying while telling myself "It's true, it's true!" Something inside me had woken up – I became aware of what had happened. But afterwards I fell back asleep. The projects arrived and I wanted to work on them. Therefore, I underwent my first psychotherapy treatment before accessing training.

One day, I saw my emotional dependency, I saw it in my drink; I knew that my emotional dependency was in the process of killing me. One morning, that's when everything happened, I saw myself in the street, I saw the little girl I once was. She was calling her boyfriend, but it wasn't her boyfriend that she really wanted, but her mother. All those years it was my mother that I was looking for, for her love, and when I finally understood that, I was then able to see my partner as a man and love him as my spouse – as a human-being. That was when I understood that the mother's love that I was deprived of as a child, I would never receive.

Today, I am doing well, I act differently than I used to, and I no longer feel attacked, humiliated or debased; I no longer feel like a destitute little girl. I am fifty years old and I have tools and abilities. Today I have turned the page, I think of my father, my mother, my brothers – I live with both my good and bad memories but I don't suffer from them. I have my son, my grandchildren, and friends – my people. There are people, always people. There is so much work left to be done to make it through. We still have to deal with both cultures for a while but our culture will prevail. We must take steps to ensure that it happens. I received a lot of western teaching in order to succeed in turning things around. That's what it took to learn about my culture; to see it clearly.

I am proud to be a First Nations member. We have survived everything we went through. I am proud of my differences, my culture that I'm increasingly in touch with. I can now differentiate the two cultures, as I can now distinguish my family life from my social life as well as my professional life. My emotions are much easier to manage now. I have attained what I wanted; I have the abilities that I wanted to have so much in the past. I can bear my culture, know it and teach it to others. Today I know what I'm doing, and I have objectives – I have broad objectives and smaller goals to reach those objectives.

My mother passed away in 2004, two days after the birth of my grandson. I was the one who was with her when she breathed for the last time.

"They say that from zero to five years of age, we learn everything we need to know to be able to function for the rest of our lives. It's our baggage for life. As for me, from one to four years of age, I gathered information on how to live as an Anishnabe and then, all of a sudden, I could no longer use the information I had collected..."

Free spirit

My name is "free spirit". My mother had me when she was only sixteen years old and gave birth to my brother when she was only fourteen. I arrived at the orphanage in La Tuque when I was four years old. Two Indians escorted us by train to the residential school before suddenly disappearing. When the nuns left with my little sister, I was really all alone. I wasn't allowed to go see my sister, she was the only family I had and lived on a floor above mine. One year later, they sent her to the *Soeurs du Bon Pasteur à Québec*. I saw her a few times afterwards. She has passed away.

At the orphanage, it was as if they had placed me in a secret area, isolated from the world, in a different and hostile universe. At night, when I went to bed, I would pull the sheets up over my head to shield myself and I would escape into my own mind - float away within my own body. That is what allowed me to avoid becoming a bad person. Sometimes, I would leave, fly away, escape from the walls and return to the North, travel over the lakes and the Saint-Maurice and then, I would realize that nobody was waiting for me elsewhere. I didn't have a place to escape to. I had the power to become a spirit in my body. I belief it's a gift I received on the reserve. I would return to my roots in order to be able to survive the next day. Healers use energy that comes from the spirit. I did this often and I still use the gift to this day.

They beat me in order to make me forget the Algonquin language. All that remains are a few snippets, almost nothing, just a few words. I learned the French language to the point where I mastered it better than the nuns. The book on my night table was the Larousse dictionary. I had perfect marks in French. When I arrived at the orphanage, I only spoke Algonquin with a touch of English. They let me know in a violent fashion that I couldn't say a word in my language. When they gave me orders in their language, I would ask them what they were saying. They thought I was being arrogant and so I got the "strap."

When I was young, I had a beautiful voice. I was a soloist in the choir for the orphanage. I sang in front of a large crowd of people in La Tuque without a microphone. My voice was very loud and in tune. They taught me the Latin Church songs and since they weren't in French, I learned them by heart, by singing and watching. When I sang at the chapel, the people recognized my voice. When I was nine years old, I had an operation for my tonsils and as of the very next day, I couldn't sing anymore.

They say that from zero to five years of age, we learn everything we need to know to be able to function for the rest of our lives. It's our baggage for life. As for me, from one to four years of age, I gathered information on how to live as an Anishnabe and then, all of a sudden, I could no longer use the information I had collected and they beat me to make me forget what I knew.

One day, they took me by car to buy shoes and then we returned to the orphanage. When the nun left, I went to the sink, turned on the tap, took off my shoes and plunged my new shoes into the water. I was beaten for doing that. For a long time, I didn't understand why I had done that. Later, I learned in a report that Indians soaked their new moccasins that were too stiff in water and then chewed on them to soften them. I had acted instinctively based on what I had learned. I also remember a lady who would bring us to a railroad in order to collect glass. At the time, I didn't understand why we were doing it but now I know it was for scraping pelts.

I was the only Aboriginal person at the orphanage. When I was seven years old, on the day of my first communion, the teacher sent us to go wash our hands and then she made us show her our hands. For the other children who were white, she said they were fine, but when I showed the teacher my hands, which were white on the inside but on the outside she said they were dirty, since they were the colour of Indians, of savages. She made me return three times to wash my hands and even ended up going to wash my hands for me. I knew that she couldn't scrub it away because I had Indian hands, but she scrubbed them until my hands were bloody.

In order to strike a balance with the suffering, oftentimes life gives us something special. I was the best at school and I was also good at games. One day, a nun said that Indians were half human and half animal. In the third grade, I wasn't good at French and I passed a test in which I barely understood anything. In grade four, I did another test and I had the highest mark. I said to others: "If I'm half animal and half human savage and I finished first - what does that make you?" The government paid for my education and that helped me a lot. I became the first Aboriginal electronic technician in Canada. At the Montreal Expo, at the Indian pavilion, there was a large photograph of me at the entrance.

I have two daughters and I feel as though things are going well with my children. I am also a grandfather. The bond with my daughters was a bit difficult to develop. Nobody showed me how, I learned by myself and I did it by myself. I tried to take the time needed to make things work. For example, one day, I spent four hours with one of my daughters devising a strategy to obtain a correct mathematical solution. My daughter was a figure skater. I would film her and then explain to her that she always had to be able to position herself in space. Today this is called mental visualization. I know that this is an Indian method that was transmitted from one human-being to another.

What helped me and continues to help me is searching for the spirit within me. When I want something, I ask the energy that is present within me. To do this, you have to close your eyes and feel the guide within. Even when I'm playing sports, I ask the spirit to guide me. The real "me" can be found there. One day, I will pass away and continue to live even if my body has returned to the earth. We pass on our gifts – to me, this energy is a genuine gift. It seems so natural this entity within me, this warmth. When I started working, whenever I was experiencing problems, I would look inside myself.

The First Peoples are starting to be recognized. I have seen several people searching for family ties with Indians in their families. I was never ashamed of being an Aboriginal person. I wondered why I was at the orphanage, but not why I was an Aboriginal. The genuine human-being is found within, in the spirit. If we can show this to our children, then we will be on the right path. We are part of the Great Spirit, we are a part of Him, He is the Chief of all of the spirits and if we can find Him within ourselves, we can also find success in our lives. Many things are still hard to grasp, unless we look within ourselves where everything is simple and real. Sometimes, we have to pass away in order to understand this dimension, understand what really exists.

At Emotions Anonymous, we can talk about our problems, our difficulties. If we talk about them, if we share them, each time we do someone takes a little bit away and it becomes more bearable. I thank those who were there for me and allowed me to express myself. Sharing and talking really helps. In my entourage, it was a taboo subject. Many people don't like to listen to those who are having problems. The melancholy is still present inside me, as if something had been taken from me when I was young. Within me, there is emptiness and it hurts when I look at it. There are things that are difficult for me;

for example, most people have parents and talk about their parents and I don't say anything. I don't have any parents, I am alone, and I am an orphan. I talk about other things when others talk about their childhood.

It is necessary to have the opportunity to be educated in order to have a beautiful life. You mustn't isolate yourself; you must find a way to live in a way to avoid it. Some of our communities are very isolated. Some of our people have nothing and they must learn how to live on their own. We must find resources in our setting that respect our culture.

I met someone whom in my eyes is the reward of an entire lifetime. Today I am happy. I have a three year old grandson and I have another grandchild on the way – and the father of this future child has asked me for my daughter's hand in marriage. My grandson has the same name as I do; it's the name that his parents gave him, even if his father already has a name, a great one. My grandson has inherited a name and an entire Aboriginal tradition.

Photo: Hemera

"Each person has a story that is worth listening to. The truth consists of talking about what we went through."

Harry

My name is Harry. I went to the Saint-Marc-de-Figuery residential school for five years.

I had a very happy childhood. We were eleven or twelve children and we lived in the forest. Back then, the Pikogan reservation didn't exist yet. Before going to the residential school, I had never seen the white man before.

My brothers and sisters went to the residential school before I did but they were forbidden to talk about it at home. I thought I was the first one on the bus; they used candy in order to encourage us to get on. When I arrived at the residential school, I was curious. I had never imagined that families could be separated. I was sad for my mother who was losing her children. The nuns talked to us about God. I didn't know who this god was, who this imaginary being was. And I put him on a pedestal. He was forced upon me and I believed in him.

I was subjected to a lot of abuse from the priests and nuns. I thought it was normal. I talked to my mother about it, because I didn't understand why the representatives of a supreme being would educate me in this way. I became revolted by the maltreatment. I was forbidden from speaking to my sisters and we were prohibited from speaking our language. I was in a constant state of anxiety; every night at bedtime I would panic. I wondered whose turn it would be that night – would it by my turn or my friends turn? Even when we were ill, we were subjected to poor treatment at the infirmary.

When I got out of the residential school, I was forbidden to discuss the abuse I was subjected to. My grandmother on my father's side was more Catholic than the pope himself. My mother believed me but she would tell me to hush up in order to avoid conflict within the family. In the classroom, the teacher didn't understand me and the white people insulted me. It would have been so easy to express myself in my language but it wasn't allowed. Therefore I quit school and returned to my community. My people had addictions issues to both alcohol and drugs. I started using very young. I was so revolted that I joined a street gang that made its own rules. I kept using until I found out that I had a very rare disease.

One day, my mother asked me to get a carton of milk and I took off for Montreal by hitchhiking. I was sixteen years old. I wanted to learn a trade, to become an electrician. My disease forced me to interrupt my training. Finally, I worked as a hairdresser in the lower St-Lawrence region. I left my community for twenty years.

When I was a young boy, we lived in the forest. Our food was adapted to my illness. Later on, when I was obligated to eat the food of the white people, I almost died from it. I am receiving treatment because I want to live. I'm not allowed to drink and its better that way; I still have too much anger inside me.

I am comfortable with discussing the abuse I was subjected to, because I was able to forgive myself. To succeed in doing so, I had to talk about what happened a lot. I was Chief in my community for fifteen years. I would tell people "Talk about it, you have to discuss it". I was stuck within my shell because I was ashamed. My mother would tell me that there was nothing to be ashamed about, because the things that happened were not my fault. I took steps to help myself outside of the community. I was the only Aboriginal person in the region I was living and I was very shy. I worked in many different trades. I travelled everywhere, particularly in Europe. I met people who were suffering the same type of pain that we were and so I started talking about my suffering. It was liberating, however there are some things that always remain inside us that eventually resurface and affect us. One day, people that I loved subjected me to violence and that was when it all came out. Whenever I thought about the violence I experienced at the residential school, it was immediately translated into violence. Whenever people would use verbal, psychological or physical violence, it all came out. Sooner or later, everything comes out.

I went to therapies. They provide you with tools but the genuine therapeutic process begins once you leave. The only thing they can really do is give you the tools. We end up accepting ourselves and thus taking a step towards healing. My faith is what saved me. That's what I really want; I want to heal and turn the page with my Creator. Faith means believing in yourself, in your capacity, in your liberation; it means living in the present rather than in the past. The past will never return. I must look at where I came from as well as where I'm going. With time, we succeed. The passage of time is important. The growth process requires time for it to happen. Regardless of what we lived through, it is necessary to take the time to set ourselves straight.

When I returned to the community, I became reacquainted with my values. I travelled and I also learned how to listen. A person who knows how to listen can learn from the wisdom of others.

I know that the Creator exists. I once spent seven months in a coma. I could hear voices around me but I was unable to communicate. When I think back on what I experienced and what I felt, I tell myself that I wish I could return to that state. Not to the extent of ending my life, because life is much too short. But when we're in a state of turmoil, life is very hard. I believe that talking about it with others is a worthy endeavour. Each person has a story that is worth listening to. The truth consists of talking about what we went through. One side of the story is never enough; we have to tell our side of the story. I love to learn but I don't like it when the learning is imposed. All peoples are entitled to learn what they want to learn. When I look at the First Nations people, I tell myself that we have to talk about what happened. The version that everyone knows makes us out to be the victims. This is dangerous. I don't want to be a victim. I can be someone who went through a terrible experience but I refuse to be a victim. I overcame these challenges. I made peace with what I went through and I believe that it's better not to dwell on it.

The unfortunate thing for the future is that the community spirit has disappeared. I have nothing against the modernity but we must not forget our culture. Our elderly people are very sensitive about modernization – they are afraid of it. We must leave our children with a heritage. The survivors must give out this information and teach the children about their past. We must unearth the suffering in order to liberate it. Our language is colourful; the youth will be able to understand what happened. We can educate them and help them to understand the government's decisions. The Indian Act was created to the detriment of Indians; it's isn't a law for Indians, it was designed to regulate Indians, just like the Indian Residential School System. Laws are made for everyone but they are difficult to fully apply. In the future, once everyone knows our story, perhaps we will succeed in changing this Act and increase awareness among people. At one point I wondered why it was that the bad side always dominates. One day, an elderly person replied to me, "It's because we accept it". Starting from the day when we will no longer accept only the bad sides of the story, we will then be able to see the good ones.

If we are seeking reconciliation, who must we reconcile with? I believe that we must reconcile with ourselves, with all parts of our being. It would be necessary, of course, to define the word reconciliation. Terrible suffering takes place in each family. Each and every one of us must take the measures that are within reach in order to appease the suffering and the violence. Everyone must take this step. In the long term, the violence will thus diminish. We have to talk about it so that things can change. When we look at what is happening in the Aboriginal communities, we see a lot of violence. Our men are violent with our women and children. Psychological and verbal violence are also part of the daily lives of our men and women.

People are fearful of words from other languages. Our language is very colourful; it is very different. When we talk to them about change, people wonder what is going to happen to them. Improvement – this is a much more positive word. In our language, we only have one word to say these things. If we were to use this word, everyone would understand. Our people would know how to react to these words that belong to them. Those who have the wisdom and those who have the power must transmit the information. Here, nearly half the community is less than 18 years of age. We must inform them. Programs exist for the youth as well as senior citizens but we often forget that those from my generation could communicate the information. There is a barrier, a gap between the generations. We tell the youth that we must preserve our language but we use the French language in order to tell them. Why don't we just talk to them in our language? I have tried it in my experiences within the community and it works. We don't have to feel sorry for ourselves while asking for money or grants. We have to take action and say what it is that we want. The money will then follow. Unfortunately, there is nothing better than money to divide a community, families and individuals. Money is stronger than everything, even stronger than our own culture.

"Today, I feel as though I'm an understanding grandmother, a good grandmother who went through many things but was able to set them aside and forgive."

Juliette

My name is Juliette Wilde. When I entered the Saint-Marc-de-Figuery residential school, I was seven years old. It was catastrophic for me. I was taken away from my parents and I didn't even know where they were bringing me.

We were five girls and two boys who went to Saint-Marc-de-Figuery out of ten children. I had my little sister named Margot with me. We left by either bus or taxi, I can't remember which, it was so far away, I don't remember how I got there but what I experienced while I was over there, I remember very well. It's as if it had all happened not so long ago. These kinds of things leave a mark and we cannot forget them. When I arrived, I was completely lost. I didn't speak French; I could only speak my Indian language. As soon as we arrived, since little girls have long hair, they cut our hair while telling us that Indians had lice. It wasn't true. I tried communicating with the nuns in order to make them understand but I wasn't able to – I could only speak my Indian language.

While I was there, I was confused as an individual, as a human-being. They told us, "If you speak your language, you will be punished. You must eat everything on your plate. Even if you don't like it, you have to eat it all." They would hit me. They would send me to bed without any dinner or I would spend the night in a dark corner as punishment.

When I was at the residential school, I thought about my parents. I missed them and even during classes, I cried. I was always thinking about them. Sometimes, they came to see us. Whenever we knew they were coming, we were so happy. It's a good thing they came to visit us or else I don't know what I would have done. I went to school there for seven years and I found it hard – so very hard. I learned to carry out orders – we walked around like soldiers. We learned to make our beds. We were assigned numbers; I was number eighty-seven.

I cannot say that I had a happy childhood. First of all, I felt like my parents had abandoned me. Now I think that they were obligated to send us to the residential school, or else the social services would have taken us away. Things like that have happened; I've read about it. If I could have been with my parents, brothers and sisters, I would have had a happy childhood. We saw each other in the summer. In the month of June we would return home – and we were so happy. Eventually, they started letting us out for Christmas, New Years and Easter. We were always happy to see our parents. Even if they had allowed us to go away, we needed them; we were very respectful of our parents. The summertime was complete joy for us but as soon as we felt the approach of the fall season, we started crying again. I didn't want to go back, but our parents didn't understand us. In their opinion, a priest or a nun could do no wrong.

I cannot say that I only experienced hardship while I was there. There were good times as well. Not all of the nuns were mean. My sisters were there as well, and I had friends. We had some good times together. At Christmas, we sang at midnight mass and then celebrated. I really enjoyed those times. Of course the food wasn't always good, but there was some good food. Such as the blanc mange for instance, I loved it, and I also enjoyed peanut butter sandwiches with hot chocolate. Its funny how there are certain little things that we'll always remember.

When I left the residential school, I must have been thirteen years old. I know that I spent seven years there. During all those years, I was taught to keep my head down. When we went to town, there were the White people and then there were the Indians. The Indians were subjected to racial segregation. They called us savages, because we were different from them. I taught them to respect me but there are some injuries that stayed with me. Everything we were told in Saint-Marc-de-Figuery became a burden that we carried around with us and as soon as someone said something negative to me, I would fall apart.

In the beginning when I started going to Rose-Anna's group, I went twice without being able to finish the sessions. However, I did go for a good part of the sessions and it helped me. It was when I went to Attitude that I told myself, "Juliette, you can express yourself, you're a good person." Before going there, I was incapable of speaking in front of people, and that was where I learned to have confidence in myself. Before then, you couldn't learn anything from me, even if you asked me questions. Today, I am well, and I'm able to express myself. I am not ashamed of myself.

When I am with my grandchildren, children, husband, brothers and sisters and we talk, those are my happiest moments. I lost a son in 1995. It took me two years to get back to living, to be able to talk about him without crying. I think about him all the time – he has been gone for thirteen years; he died on a February 28th. The months of February are very hard on me. I went and got the help that I needed from a psychologist. I also have another boy and two daughters, and six grandchildren. I had a lot of problems with addictions but I didn't know why I was drinking so much. Today, I am well because I've overcome my addictions. It's possible to enjoy a nice glass of wine without losing control of your life.

The things we went through at Saint-Marc-de-Figuery, we kept inside ourselves for a long time, and we didn't want to talk about them because we were ashamed. I had an unhappy childhood because I didn't have my parents. I was confused, humiliated and beaten. I experienced brutality – and other things as well. When I went with Rose-Anna, it helped me a lot. When we are in the group, we can talk about anything; there is nothing to be ashamed of. It is important to talk about it so that the healing process can take place. We were afraid to talk about it; we would have liked to talk about it with our parents. The best way to set it all aside is to discuss it with a trustworthy person. Going to Attitude was an eye-opening experience for me. It lasted for five days, in silence, and we couldn't see each other. I even discussed my residential school experience while I was there. They asked me to write a letter regarding what I went through at Saint-Marc-de-Figuery and I didn't leave anything out. I just let it all out and it felt good. It made me understand. Something changed: before then I was so angry with them and today, that is no longer the case. I tell myself that they are the ones with something to be ashamed of, not me. I resent them, and it's normal, but not to the point where I'll spend my time hating them for the rest of my life. I have my own world inside me and evil has no place there.

It is necessary to talk about it, to open ourselves up. I didn't know that I was so resentful, so full of bitterness. When I left Attitude, I felt like I was flying, I felt lighter, and I didn't want to return home. The past returns to me less often nowadays. I don't talk about it with my children. My daughters came with me when I went to the hearing. Before then, they hadn't known what I had gone through. But we don't talk about it anymore. They don't ask me questions. All of my children are aware but they don't ask me anything. I must return to a hearing shortly and I will invite my daughters to come with me.

I experienced the residential schools and when I got out, I told myself, "Never will my children go there. I will never send my children to a residential school." Today, I feel as though I'm an understanding grandmother, a good grandmother who went through many things but was able to set them aside and forgive. The message that I'd like to relay to my grandchildren would be the following: "Grandma went through some things that were not always fun. Today, you are comfortable, you are well surrounded, well cared for, you go to school, you have food on the table and clothing. Take advantage of it all. Learn to live life one day at a time."

It was necessary to invent ways to teach children to trust adults with the experiences that we had. We tell them, "Don't talk to strangers!", "Don't go with strangers!", "Be wary of others, not all people are good people!", "Don't stay in places where people are drinking!" and "If you come to my home, grandma is always there for you!" I send them messages. The youth mustn't be left to their own devices. The messages must be relayed in a way that ensures that they understand them. We must remain vigilant.

"They must put themselves back together and they use all sorts of tools in order to eliminate the anger and the defeatism ingrained into the little girls, now that they have become women."

Lisette
Saint-Marc-de-Figuery residential school

You could say that I was fortunate enough to have a childhood. I went to the residential school when I was eleven years old.

Before, Pikogan didn't exist here. This village didn't exist. My family lived here – there was a single home and it was the family home. My parents raised me in the forest. I experienced childhood; I experienced the joy of living with my parents and they were the ones who raised me. So at eleven years old when I left for the residential school, I felt as though I was torn away from them. We left in the fall season for the residential school and only returned in the month of June. It's incredible, the impact that it had on my life. Everything I knew was immediately taken from me, from my childhood joys to our language. We were not allowed to speak our language. It was very difficult.

We were five girls and two boys from the same family who went to the residential school. In terms of our ages, we were born one after the other.

When you are abused and then later try to make your place in the world and live your life, you transmit that abuse. Aggressiveness; I had a lot of it pent up inside me. The nuns would pull our ears and our hair. We were told to kneel and then they told us that our parents were dirty and that we had lice. I found it to be very difficult but I nonetheless adapted. I learned things. I even learned good things, for instance I can write and communicate – I received an education. I am happy that I did even though the environment in which I received that education was so negative.

I attended the residential school until the age of fifteen years. That was my last year there. I didn't like what was going on at the school. I saw so many things, I heard so many things, and I no longer wanted to stay there. You understand what's going on, you are aware of what's happening but you feel powerless. When I got out of the residential school I felt numb, in a daze, because of everything I had inside me. I didn't even talk about it. I was beaten and punched but I was never sexually abused. When the priest tried to touch us during confession, I got very angry and told him, "No, I won't let you touch me!" And nobody ever did.

Around me I had my friends, I had my sisters, but I was always afraid of what was going to happen. I was really worried because of the things I was hearing, because of the things that could be going on. We heard strange noises during the night. There were five dormitories. My friends and I, we never discussed what we heard or what we saw. We were too scared; we tried to block it out.

As for me, it was my anger that protected me. There were many little girls who were sexually assaulted. Some of my sisters were abused. For all of those who were sexually abused, it took them a lot of time to get it together again. They must put themselves back together and use all sorts of tools in order to eliminate the anger and the defeatism ingrained into the little girls, now that they have become women. I know women who still tell me to this day how horrifying it was for them. Just being physically beaten was horrifying. I would run away, it was a matter of survival; we had to get away but they would always end up catching us.

Moreover, our parents didn't believe us, but I can't place the blame on my parents' shoulders. They just couldn't believe that what we were telling them was true. I remember throwing massive fits in order to avoid returning to the residential school; I cried, I did anything I could, but they were still the ones in control; I was still a minor.

While hoping that I would heal and get better, I left everything on the backburner for a long time. When I no longer had any choice but to start taking care of it, there were a lot of problems in the community related to alcohol and drugs. I knew that something was obviously going on. We talked amongst ourselves and people started telling each other more and more things. I heard and I listened to people. What led me to making the decision to do something was when I started having grandchildren. That's when I said to myself, "You have to start with yourself before you can transmit the nice things in life to others." I will always remember that point in my life. And yet, everything that I did made life more difficult. I drank. One day, I asked myself, "Hey, what's going on with me?" I wanted to teach my children and give them a sense of identity, but I understood that I had to start by taking care of myself.

In order to be able to transmit good things to them, I had to do some work inside myself. It was so deeply rooted within me. I knew that the aggression that I kept inside had been my only defence mechanism at the time.

I never spoke to my children about the residential school experience. They figured that it was alright since I never talked about it. Despite everything, I still managed to transmit good values to them. They are hard workers. I didn't want my grandchildren to see me drinking in an excessive manner. I wanted to teach them moderation in all things. Not everyone goes through the same things, and everyone sees things differently.

We were fortunate to have people around who took care of us. We have developed a nice relationship with Rose-Anna and Julie, with those who were around us during the healing process. It was nice to be able to talk about it, to finally share what had happened to us. Finally, we could free ourselves from our shells, from everything that we pretended didn't happen for so long. That is so exciting to me.

I even went on a retreat in St. Jérôme. It was a fulfilling experience. It was facilitated by a priest, an oblate who taught us and it was a great experience. That was when I understood that not all religious people were necessarily the same. The priest admitted to what had happened in the residential schools. He talked to us about God and forgiveness. That provided some reconciliation in terms of what was really bothering me. I am a spiritual person. I go to church; I see it as an opportunity to collect myself by taking a step back and reflecting on things. I don't go to church for the priests who caused us so much pain.

As much as we once believed that we were responsible for the things that happened to us, today I understand that we must do something to help ourselves. Not to help others, but to help ourselves. I have the impression that we lived our lives a lot for others, because that's what we learned through the Catholic religion. Those who helped us brought us to understand that we shouldn't feel guilty for thinking about ourselves. I am on the path to healing. I really mean that and today I only want to carry positive things around with me.

Today, the nicest times are times of healing; just being able to heal and accepting others for who they are, without judging them. This leads to success. Things like loving your neighbour, appreciating people and having good times. I can do these things because I took control of my life.

My children see the path that I travelled. I wasn't easy on my children – I wanted to control everything. I was controlled and I wanted to control everything in turn. I am happy today because I can communicate with them; I can ensure their well-being without always fighting with them, or being on the defensive for some reason or another. I would like to thank those who listen to me - people such as Rose-Anna. I have allowed myself to shed some tears. I still have the will to persevere and pass things on – to teach good values to my children. That's what's important.

Today, I hope that as First Nations people we can live in harmony: for each of us to do our part so that we can live in harmony with the things we have – our language, our culture and our grandchildren. Our grandchildren are very important. We must guide them well. It takes time to rebuild that which has been destroyed. The residential schools tore us apart, but we must put ourselves back together now.

When I was younger I didn't want anyone to know that I was an Indian. I was ashamed; it was programmed, ingrained within me. At fifteen years of age that wasn't a problem anymore. I didn't talk about the residential school anymore and I quickly integrated myself into the lifestyle of the White people. However, after I got married, I regained my pride and I was no longer ashamed to tell people that I was an Indian. I could show them that I was a good person, that we were a good people. I am someone who always wants good things and I'm ready to fight for the things that I want. But I no longer fight by attacking others; I'm finished with attacking others. To achieve what I want, I know that I must work hard and that I must also listen to others to facilitate the task.

Hope emerges once we understand that there is a way to achieve healing: it is necessary to get the help and tools needed to work on one's personal growth. There are a lot of resource people available; it is important to persevere, not get discouraged, look within ourselves and accept that we are good people. It is important to take control over our lives and be aware of the fact that our lives belong to us. It's our own responsibility to offer ourselves a good life, a nice future, for ourselves and for our children.

One day, I was watching a television show with Dolly Dimitrio. Someone had had a discussion with her regarding the *maison des Jésuites*, the *maison Attitude*. Many people had gone there and I told myself that it might be good for me too. I had already considered participating in personal growth workshops. These types of workshops provide help in terms of asking the right questions regarding the things that are happening inside us. As I previously mentioned, everything had remained dormant inside of me for a long time, but once it awakened, there was no end to it. The more I progressed, the more help I needed for my healing process. The psychologist understood what we were going through.

There are so many wounds in this community. I've often heard people say things like "Why does my father drink?" That's what's being transmitted; the youth are wondering what's going on, and we must listen to them, and if they wish to learn, then they must participate and they must also listen to those who are trying to heal. If you really want to heal you have to start by understanding. They must hear about the suffering and help those who are affected by it. I used to isolate myself because I didn't want others to know, but today, I am happy when others come to see me because it helps me and it also helps them at the same time. That is the story I wanted to share with you: we must teach our children who we are while being proud of what we are.

What does a happy childhood mean? It means having supportive care and attention from good parents, to ensure that we go to school and get a good education; to participate with us in activities that we find interesting, such as sports. That's what I do. Since he was four years old, my grandson has played hockey and ever since he started, I've watched him play. Today, he is in midget *espoir* hockey. My husband and I used to wake up early in the morning in order to drive him to his games. I often talk to my children about how important it is. It is necessary to get involved with our children, it's important to participate in their fulfillment, and to surround them with love. These are the essentials: shelter, food and love.

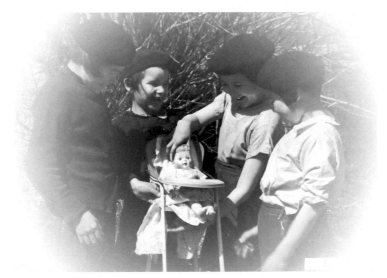

Photo: Istock

"What I wanted the most is what we are doing today: not complaining but rather informing others that we missed out on the essentials and went through difficult situations."

Marguerite

I use both names and I'm an Atikamekw from Wemotaci.

I felt that I needed to change something in my life when I started having addictions issues. I already had two children when I separated and that was when I started having problems. A few years later I understood that I needed to stop. I could see that I was hurting my children. I was there, but at the same time I was absent. My husband was there, but our children were alone. I never had a family life and yet here I was depriving my children from our presence. I looked inside myself; I asked myself some important questions and I understood that seeing their parents drinking wasn't in the best interests of my children's lives.

Other people who were going through the same things as me had started opening up and that was what got me to talk about my experience at the residential schools for the first time. For me, it was at the cultural level that I had suffered the most loss. I refused to go into the forest with my family, and I hated sleeping on the ground. Today, with my husband, we love nature; we go fishing and we go camping; in fact, we do what our parents were doing back in the day. It was because of the stories that my uncle told us that we developed the desire to do as they did. He told us about how they lived back in the day. They were a nomadic people. While travelling, they randomly encountered other communities and they would camp out together. I started going into the forest with children during the cultural week that is integrated into the school curriculum and we lived as our ancestors once did.

For a while, I was shy about being an Aboriginal person. At the residential school, they said that we were dirty, lazy and alcoholic. I wanted to prove that I wasn't like that. I regained my self-confidence when we built the school in our community and white teachers came to teach. I appreciated them, I was comfortable with them, and we would go on outings together and have picnics. They appreciated us as well and that was how I got over my shyness. Now, I am comfortable when I go into town; I greet people I don't know. That's how we create connections with others. I approach them; I would like people to recognize that we are not savages.

My greatest source of pride is having gone into Europe to teach others about my culture. I was delegated in order to go talk about my village, language, culture and arts and crafts and it filled me with a sense of pride. The French have a deep appreciation for the works of Aboriginal people. I like to visit other continents to talk about my Nation. Today, we receive more and more invitations. Before, we were simply forgotten.

I am very proud to be an Atikamekw, to be Aboriginal. I am proud to have been able to preserve my culture and language and to speak it at home with my children and grandchildren.

I was two years old when I lost my mother. I was placed in a foster family and the person who cared for me taught me everything and that is why I'm able to get by today. Narcisse Coocoo and his wife Emma had a huge impact on my life. They taught me about respect and tolerance. Once, they said to me, "If you have nothing at home besides bannock and tea, place a tablecloth on the ground and offer it to those who come to see you." I often repeat that to my children. They were like a mother and father to me. They had already passed away by the time I got married but they will always remain in my heart.

When I got out of the residential school, I must have been nine years old. My father had gotten remarried and I had preferred to live with Narcisse. Afterwards, I went to the residential school in Abitibi for five years and then I went to Pointe-Bleue for another year. Did I have a happy childhood? I had a happy childhood despite the fact that I was an orphan. My family connections were severed because of the residential schools but I also learned a lot while I was there: knitting, sewing, and cooking – the essentials to get by without going shopping.

When I saw the things that were happening to our children, it reminded me of what had happened at the residential school and that was when I started sensing the need to talk about it. I was subjected to violence from the teachers; I was beaten. I had never talked about it before. I didn't know who I could talk about it to and those I tried to discuss it with quickly changed the subject of conversation. I kept everything inside me. I should have taken control sooner because there are times when it still haunts me, hurts me, disturbs me. I lost many things. I lost my father and I could have learned so much from him.

Today I am happy. We have now reached the fourth generation. I am happy despite what we are seeing in our communities. We are trying our best to remain healthy. My children check in on me to see how I'm doing and they visit me. I take care of them as well. Nowadays, all of the houses are the same both inside and outside. It seems like we never leave our homes. We should be outside planting trees, decorating our homes differently, and just generally getting away from each other a bit. If we did these things, violence would not happen as regularly.

I tell the youth today not to give up. There is always someone out there who has a solution and it isn't necessarily someone in the family. There are people who are trustworthy and willing to welcome us with open arms. All one needs to do is go see them. That's what I did when I was suffering. There are always good people willing to listen; they are always ready to understand, to provide comfort. We are never really alone.

I haven't been connected with Aboriginal spirituality for a long time because I was raised in Christian faith and I was comfortable there. I had learned that there were meetings organized in order to get closer to nature. I participated and I learned what was good for me. One day, I was asked if I wanted to purify a home that would serve as a location for meetings. I went to ask permission. They told me, "Go ahead. If they asked you, it's because they trust you. Do it." I purified the home with a feather and sage. I also purified a drum. It is important not to let our Elders pass away without learning everything we can from them. During a meeting, they made an observation regarding the increasing number of strollers they were seeing. "We don't see the kinwagen, the baby-carrier, anymore. Why don't you undertake the responsibility of transmitting this knowledge, this tradition?" And so that's what I'm doing.

I am still very close to my children and I'm always available for them. For as long as I'm able to do help them in their lives, I will continue doing so. I loved having children. I love children. I accept children who are being placed, but today they tell me that I've gotten older and that I must let the parents take care of them. Time passes slowly when we are home alone. My children work and my grandchildren go to school.

I have only recently started participating in activities that are related to the residential schools or the sharing sessions. They have helped me. Some people are very strong and have managed to get through it. I told myself that I was also able to overcome my shortcomings resulting from the residential schools. What I wanted the most is what we are doing today: not complaining but rather informing others that we missed out on the essentials and went through difficult situations. We came out with some issues, and some of us were unable to recover from what we were subjected to and therefore aren't with us today to talk to us about their experiences. That's what I would like to see: survivors mutually helping each other to become stronger.

My husband and I went to see what remained of the Saint-Marc-de-Figuery residential school on our own initiative without asking anyone. We went beside the church in the place we would gather. I didn't know that it had been destroyed. If I saw the nuns and priests today perhaps I'd wait for them to come to me, or perhaps I'd see them through the eyes of little Marguerite who was always waiting for someone to hold her. They never held us in their arms. I would like to hear what they have to say for themselves. There was a nun who helped in the preparations for community celebrations who I really liked. I called her my very close sister. She is retired now, at the *maison-mère de Val d'Or.* There are some good nuns; I haven't put them all in one basket.

When I took control over my life, I needed help. I had to return for help twice, since I had fallen back down again. After that, I reflected on things. I reminded myself that I knew what needed to be done. But I had lost my tools. I went to a therapy centre for Aboriginal people. It felt like a family had come to get me. A few days before going there, I had picked up a doll that was abandoned in the street by dogs. I remembered that I had been picked up that way as well. I washed the doll and dried it. I was leaving for therapy the next day. I dressed the doll and put her on my bed. Before leaving, I told her to wait for me, that I would return. I talked to her as if I was talking to little Marguerite. It was the same doll that an intervener had presented to me in therapy. It was my wish when I was a little girl that someone would hold me in their arms. And so I talked to her and rocked her and loved her. Before that, I didn't love Marguerite – I didn't love her as a mother or as a wife. Today, I appreciate myself as a woman, as a mother and as a grandmother. Here, in the community, people ask me for help and it gives me strength. I want to be a role model for others; I want to be a good person.

At the residential school, we weren't allowed to have our own toys. I received my first doll at fifty years of age. My mother offered me my first doll at fifty years old.

Photo: Patrice Gosselin

"It was a closed wound that remained dormant with clenched fists, and I told myself, I'm going to open the wound, I'm going to talk about it and get rid of this wound that is so deeply cut within me. When I gave my testimony, it was very hard. I suffered a great deal, but that was when the healing process began."

Marguerite

My name is Marguerite Wilde and I'm from the community of Pikogan. I am an Algonquin and I attended the Saint-Marc-de-Figuery Indian residential school starting in 1957. I was seven years old when I started school there. When I got in, I believe I was the fifth person in the family to go to the residential school. I had no prior knowledge of the residential school; my sister didn't talk to me about it and so I left Clova, left my family, for unknown horizons. I was happy to go too. I couldn't speak a word of French – I could only speak my Algonquin language.

When I got there, it felt as if I had been struck with a hammer. I was completely isolated, lost in my environment and I couldn't find my sisters. We were in the same building and yet I had no contact with them. When we arrived there they made us wear different clothing and they cut our hair. I think that's what scared me the most; I had long, braided hair upon my arrival. When they cut my hair, a square cut, it was like I was being radically torn from my world, as if I was losing my nation, my identity. Even the sound of the razor was terrifying to me.

I was number one hundred and sixteen. I was trying to find myself; I was lost. It felt like I had been placed in a black garbage bag that was sealed. Everything was black, completely black to my eyes and I wondered if I was the only one to feel that way, to be in that state of mind. When you lose everything, you become nothing. Nothing is the same. I was looking for my sisters while using my language but we were forbidden to speak our language. We were prohibited from speaking it because they couldn't understand it. And then, little by little, it was like discovering a different world. They placed us in rows, all in a line, and we had to follow instructions. For the first weeks of classes, my cousins and I recognized each other, we were raised together, and none of us could understand anything. We were taught by nuns. One time I was so afraid, I remember it well. This short, stocky nun was so angry that she was rolling on the ground, red with rage, because we couldn't understand anything. She was trying to teach us and we couldn't understand. She showed us pictures, such as pictures of vegetables for example, but we didn't know the corresponding word. Little by little, we did end up understanding the language.

We communicated amongst ourselves in secret in the schoolyard during recess. When the monitor moved away, we would hurry. It was also during recess that we would gather - the Atikamekw were together and the Algonquin were together. We avoided mixing with the others at first. We didn't mix at all. Surrounded by our cousins, we were in our own little world. It was the only opportunity we had to speak our language because as soon as we were back in class, it was forbidden. If they caught us they would shame our culture. That was what the assimilation process was like. We were children; we were pure children. In my eyes, there was no such thing as sin. Also, in our culture, looking our parents in the eyes was an insult for them. When our mother spoke to us, never would we have dared to stare at her. Whereas the nuns would tell us, "Look at me when I'm talking to you." That just wasn't part of our culture. For us, even if we kept playing, we could still hear when someone was talking to us. Learning among Indians is mostly achieved through observation – as is respect. We didn't ask any questions such as how or why. For them, it was necessary to be looking at the teacher. It was the exact opposite. We are familiar with the concept now, but our mentality remains the same to this day since it is a part of our culture. Often, when we talk to someone, we look elsewhere. Our parents, when they educated us, they would never raise their voice. I never heard my mother raise her voice. The nuns always raised their voices and it scared us!

When I got out of the residential school in 1964, we always hung out among Aboriginals; we had no more contact with White people. For my last year at the residential school, I didn't want to go back there. We told our parents the things that happened at the residential school but they didn't believe us. And so I said to my mother, "I don't want to go back there." When the time came to go back to school, my sister and I ran off into the forest and hid for an entire day. I must have been twelve or thirteen years old. Then, we went to a different school with non-Aboriginal people. There, we spoke French, but we didn't mix with others. At first I was shy, but I was able to preserve my language. They called us "squaws." In my class, I was alone and so I kept to myself since I didn't understand their culture.

I attended the residential school until high school. Then I worked a little bit in the communities on various projects. I got married and had three boys that I was tough on while I raised them. It was similar to when I was at the residential school; I was very strict. I never talked about the residential school with my children or my husband. My husband also went to a residential school. He was in the same class as I was and we were both abused. Together, we decided that we would never discuss the residential school – that it would be buried with us once we both passed away. I started talking about it with my children only once my husband passed away.

Whenever I went to town and passed by the residential school, it always had an effect in my heart. When I provided my testimony on the Point program on *Radio Canada* in 2004, I let my children know. I allowed them to watch it but not at our home. It was like opening myself up. It was a closed wound that remained dormant with clenched fists and I told myself, I'm going to open the wound, I'm going to talk about it and get rid of this wound that is cut so deeply within me. When I gave my testimony, it was very hard. I suffered a great deal, but that was when the healing process began. I had been hearing about it since the year 2000 and I was starting to consider it. We asked ourselves questions, I needed to know why I was the way that I was – I needed to understand both for myself and for my children. Talking about it was what helped me the most. At first, many people in the communities would say, "Why talk about it?" It was such a taboo subject for our parents. It was considered taboo since it was related to the priests. They were the ones who managed the residential schools back in the day. When I started opening up, it gave me a sense of being liberated– particularly when I started working with Rose-Anna.

And then there were our parents. My mother understands French well. So, when I gave my testimony, I called my mother and asked her "Mom, did you understand what I said?" She answered that she did understand and that she had never thought it to be that way. It had the impact of a bomb being dropped. Afterwards, following a request from the band council, I provided my testimony for Women's Day in the month of March. I spoke to the Elders. Many Elders came to see me in order to speak with me. I was worried about hurting them and so I told them not to feel guilty. They had nothing to feel guilty about; it was the government's fault. Our parents never told us the effect it had on them, having their children taken away from them to be placed in a residential school. They never spoke about the sadness that they experienced. Now we are starting to talk about these things. We performed situation scenarios with psychologists. I believe that we have to do our best to try to feel well. We suffered injuries, we have to be able to forgive and we have to be able to go on with our lives.

For starters, I told myself that I was going to make something out of my life and so I turned towards teaching. I got my certificate and then my bachelor's degree. I can say that I succeeded and I'm very pleased. I taught in my community for twenty-eight years - in nursery school, kindergarten as well as grades three and four of elementary school. Then, I taught language and culture in three components:

pedagogy, arts and crafts and traditional food. I love it, in fact, I'm still teaching it today. I base my teaching on the child's rhythm. I listen to the Aboriginal children without aggravating them and it helps me.

Our Elders also teach us a lot. My mother taught me how to write and how to preserve our culture and our language. I believe that the Elders are very important in our community and we must be aware of the need to listen to them. They have something to show us every day. They transmit their gifts to us, their ways of doing things and their spirituality. It is necessary to be receptive of their teachings and respect their entourage. There are few Elders remaining in our community. My mother-in-law is specialized in medicinal plants. She still works with these plants with her daughter Rose-Anna. My mother and my mother-in-law make a lot of arts and crafts; it was my mother-in-law who showed me how. She is patient and optimistic and she thus fosters success.

Now, I'm doing very well. I've been through therapies and today I'm unable to talk about what happened. I am filled with more hope now. There are still many people who are unable to open themselves up. However, in the other communities, there are more and more people who are opening up to us. There are even those who come and see us in order to ask us what we think about the residential schools, how we managed to deal with what happened and just to have a discussion. They also want to know how our working group started. We started small by facilitating small workshops.

For the past four years, we have held sharing sessions with the four generations. For the upcoming generations, we must leave them with our history so that they all know our genuine history. We must also transmit our culture, knowledge and the stories of our Elders. We must spend time with the Elders, as this is essential to the preservation of our language, our culture, our religion and respect for who we are. All of these things are important. I am now in touch with my Aboriginal spirituality. When I wake up each day, I give thanks for the beautiful day; I thank the Creator for having the opportunity to learn for another day. I provide testimonies, participate in sharing sessions and even visit universities. They thank us and are better able to understand us by opening up to our culture and our history.

Photo: FNQLHSSC

Collection of life stories of the survivors of the Quebec Indian Residential Schools

Photo: Istock

"In my readings I came across a passage that said we don't become old simply because we've lived a given number of years, but rather because we have neglected our dreams. My dream was to return home."

Richard
Wemotaci

My name is Richard Niquay and I'm from the community of Wemotaci. I attended two residential schools in my life. In 1958 and 59, I went to Saint-Marc-de-Figuery and in 1960, in the month of October, the young Atikamekw children left for the Pointe Bleue residential school. I returned there nine times. I spent eleven years of my life in residential schools. There were nineteen children in my family; I believe we were one of the biggest families in the community and almost all of us went to the residential schools.

The first time I noticed that my life was undergoing a drastic change, in fact, the greatest change of my life, was when I left the lands we were living on. Up to the age of seven years old, I lived on our lands. My father hunted and trapped; he showed us how to live in nature, how to live in the forest. In September of 1958, I took the train in Parent in order to go to the residential school. I felt the change in my life while riding the train and then the bus. During the journey, I felt an increase in solitude, sadness and vulnerability. That was when I noticed that something was going on, even though I was eager to get to the residential school. I already had a sister and a brother who had gone there for one or two years. When I got off the train in Amos, we took the bus and I remember crying during the ride. There was a child from Obedjiwan who must have been one or two years older than me who gave me coins to console me and he said to me, "Don't cry, have some coins, there's no need to cry."

The buses stopped in front of the residential school and when I got off, I understood that the changes in my life would be even greater than I had ever imagined. We entered a large hall and there were lockers on three sides of the room. Everyone was assigned a locker and on each locker there was a number. The number was my identification, I was now a number, and from that point on my socks, my shirts and my pants were marked with this number. They then told us to put our personal belongings in our lockers.

I was worried; I didn't really understand what was happening to me. I also didn't know that I would be spending ten months there. I thought I would be leaving the following week.

I didn't really like living in a group, I was obligated to follow the group as well as the rules in the dormitories and in the classrooms. I wasn't familiar with regulations; I didn't have any back home. Today I understand that regulations are essential to harmony and collaboration when living in a group. But over there, the regulations were very strict. When, for the first time, I saw an older student being severely punished, I started feeling that I had to follow the rules in order to avoid being kicked or getting my ears pulled. I noticed that there was something wrong - the punishments were always blown out of proportion.

I liked school and I was a good boy, even when I was on my land. At the residential school, you're far away from home in an unfamiliar place with strangers who you get to know and who are in the same boat as you - who become your friends and companions. We protected each other. We had a social life; we lent each other personal belongings such as comic books. I started enjoying reading and I read many books. I started with short comics and after that I read more serious books. At Pointe Bleue, I read all of the Bob Morane books. My teacher gave me another reading suggestion and so reading became a means of escape – a source of freedom. I learned to read and write. It helped me to forget that I wasn't happy at the residential school.

I was never happy at the residential school. I had enuresis problems – nobody explained to me that it's a psychological and physical problem. They thought that I would best learn and understand by receiving the belt.

The two years I spent in Amos were the worst in terms of disorientation. They didn't teach us to be proud of our origins or our Nation. They taught us things that were in no way connected with our way of life, of thinking – with our spirituality. Regardless, everything that I did learn, I wish I could have learned in different conditions.

In Pointe Bleue, whenever I got out of the residential school, all I could see was a large lake, which was St. Jean Lake. I would have preferred a smaller lake with a cabin – a home. I dreamed of living in a small world – to return home - to escape all of the rules. In the fall, things were really hard but when springtime arrived along with the dreams of summer vacation, I was vibrant and life was really good. I returned home to our lands. My family lived in a log cabin during the winter but during the summertime, we camped out by the lakes and we hunted moose. We would kill two moose just for our family and then we would give some to others. All throughout the summer, we lived together. My sisters lived with my mother at the camp. My father, my brothers and I would sometimes set out in a canoe and sleep under the stars.

Once, later in the summer, we went camping closer to Abitibi. There had been a large forest fire and a lot of blueberry bushes had grown. We went blueberry picking for two weeks, just before returning to the residential school. Whenever I started thinking about returning to the residential school, I became stressed out and didn't feel well – I couldn't sleep anymore and I stopped eating.

My father and mother knew nothing about the books that I brought home from school. I never had any dreams for my future, any professional ambition. I would only tell myself that as soon as I was done with the residential school, I would return home. And that's exactly what I did. In better conditions, I would have studied more. In my readings I came across a passage that said that we don't become old simply because we've lived a given number of years, but rather because we have neglected our dreams. My dream was to return home.

Towards the end of the 1960s, I bought myself a chainsaw in order to cut wood. An Indian Affairs agent helped us purchase saws. He provided seventy or seventy-five dollars towards a chainsaw that was worth two hundred and fifty and we had the rest of the summer to pay off the rest.

Some years, I was first in my class and then one day, I dropped out of school. In 1977, I returned to school but I left one week later. I wanted to see the principal, but instead I met a priest who didn't like us and he asked me if I had a heart since I wasn't using it for my studies. I told that to my teacher. I told him that I wasn't comfortable and that I had never been happy. He asked me if I had any money, but I didn't have any money. So he told me, "I'll loan you some. Tonight you can come and eat at my home. You can spend your evening at my place while waiting for the train. My mother will also give you some money." She did give me money, and all she asked for in return was that I pray for her. I returned home to join my father in the forest in the log cabin and I spent the rest of the winter there. The following fall, I had to return to the residential school once again.

My experiences at the residential schools occasionally return to me at times such as Easter. Our parents were allowed to visit us but mine rarely came. I remember one year Easter had passed and a priest gathered us into a large room and spoke to us about our fathers and mothers in a way that I didn't appreciate. They wanted us to be ashamed of our parents. I couldn't believe that this was coming from the priests – from those who were always talking about Christian charity. I had much to share at the hearing.

When the residential school was over for me, I worked in Quebec and I met my future wife, a *Québecoise*. I have a boy who is thirty-four years old today. My marriage lasted five years. I couldn't explain what it was, but I was always carrying something around with me and I didn't know what it was. One day, I was no longer able to work, I was unable to tell people about my past, and I started crying. The doctor advised me to see a psychologist but I didn't want to be locked away. And so I carried my burden around with me and when I separated, everything came tumbling down. I signed up for assembly line worker training and during the course, I went through a depression. I saw then that I had accumulated all sorts of pain, frustrations and fears. I followed at least twenty-five therapies during my life for alcohol and drug use and each time I told my story. It wasn't these therapy sessions that truly helped me. Each time I was finished, I was able to function for nine months. I called these my novena.

The thing that helped me the most were the trips I took out west. These trips gave me the opportunity to reconnect with the culture that I had lost along the way. I am becoming increasingly involved with spirituality. I learned to look at myself, to respect myself, to trust myself – to learn my value as a human-being. At the residential school, we never had a say in anything, we had to listen to the priests. The thing that helped me when I went out west was the sense of freedom. I performed two sweat lodges per day, with people who spoke my language and practiced my spirituality. I am going back next summer. I am becoming a more spiritual person – and more patient as well, and I'm more willing to accept. It's like a gift, a benediction. I have gotten back in touch with my identity.

Today, we are in a period of reflection. With the Healing Foundation, we think about what happened to us, we realize that we experienced certain things in the past. But now, they give us tools and we must take them. We must give ourselves the best chances of regaining our pride, to be ourselves around others – it's a struggle that we're fighting together. We must tell ourselves that thankfully it's in the past, that we made it through it all while demonstrating our strength and resilience. That's what the post-residential school experience is all about.

I would like to ask the communities to open their eyes and not be afraid to look to the past to live in the present, because there is much positive to be found in the future. We can't change the things that have happened but we can work together so that our children and grandchildren can see that we nonetheless persevered. It's not because we lived for a certain number of years at the residential school that we have to be sad for the rest of our lives.

I live my role as a grandfather in my mind because my children live far away from me. I am proud of them – they don't touch alcohol or drugs. It helps my healing process when I see my daughter take care of her children without drinking or using drugs. She made me older, I became a grandfather, and now my hope is that my grandchild will never have to go to a residential school. But will he want to go to school? One thing is certain - I will try to instil the desire to read in him because it helps a lot – reading was my salvation.

I was never ashamed of being an Aboriginal person even if at the residential school they almost succeeded. My ancestors gave me strength and patience. The future generations will be fortunate because there are so many people who are trying to wake up and they are realizing that there are things to do that must be accomplished. Our children will have to be proud of us. Even if what we leave them with will not be intact, it will be in a good state. There is a need for more funding to ensure the continuation of the healing activities or else we won't be able to finish what we started. We must ensure that the things that happened are remembered. I wonder if Canadians really want to hear the truth. There are still those who deny the history of the residential schools.

Photo: Hemera

"Today, people want to know even more about themselves. It is true that the more we talk about ourselves, the more we come out of our shell. We are then no longer the victim, we are free."

Rose-Anna

We were ten children in our family and only my two youngest brothers never went to a residential school. Four members of my family were in the residential school at the same time the year it opened. The thing I'd like to know today is why I can't remember my departure for the residential school or my arrival there – I can't remember a thing. I remember all the little girls crying around me and I recall telling myself, "What's going on?" That was when I woke up.

I was nine years old when I first went to the residential school, so I remember quite clearly when we used to live in the forest. My grandmother was there, as were my parents. I learned about arts and crafts and daily chores at a young age. We learned how to live and be responsible. I was disobedient when I was young. For instance, my father would tell me, "I don't want you to go down by the shore" and yet I would always sneak off to go by the water. One day, they were watching me as I went to the water and I fell in. I didn't know I was being watched. My father immediately came to my rescue. That was how we learned.

Contact with the nuns was very difficult, we couldn't understand each other. A nun would ask me to repeat a word and I'd say it all wrong. I had no idea what was going on. We were all assigned a number – they didn't called me Rose-Anna; they called me sixty-three. It was my number. They never referred to us by name. We were often punished for simply not understanding.

As soon as we arrived at the residential school, we were forbidden to speak the Algonquin language. They would beat us if they caught us speaking our language to each other. We spoke only in French. Therefore, our parents would let us know that we had really become separated from them, that we no longer had any contact with them. They would say to us, "You're Indians, speak your Indian language. We can't understand you." As time passed, when we returned to our families, we could no longer communicate with our parents. We didn't speak the same language.

Of course, there were times when we had fun – we were children after all. I loved to go sliding and skating. We were obligated to stay outside but there were activities that we enjoyed. At recess time, we would fight each other since we weren't all from the same Nation. When we arrived, there were many Atikamekw children – it took quite some time before we became friends with them. Later on, amongst ourselves, we spoke the Atikamekw language.

The first time we arrived at the dormitory and I saw my little bed, I was afraid of falling off. I placed my blanket underneath me because I was afraid there might be someone under the bed. We were a nomadic people, and as such I had never slept in a bed before. We slept in tents for ten months at a time in the forest. I found the bed to be quite uncomfortable. There were many little beds with no space between them and many children around me.

One day, I no longer wanted to return to the residential school. I did everything I could to avoid staying there. My cousin and I were forced to mend socks, but we weren't given needles. Therefore, we weren't able to mend the socks and we were punished for it. The nun brought us before the principal. We waited on our knees and the head priest came and gave my cousin the strap right beside me. And so I told myself, "No, you will not hurt me, I won't let you hurt me." And when it was my turn to get the strap, it didn't hurt; I didn't feel a thing. It was as if I was numb and so I laughed at him. They called our parents at one o'clock in the morning. We told them what had happened. The nuns no longer wanted anything to do with us and expelled us from the residential school. I was thirteen years old at the time.

The following year, I went to St. Thérèse School with a different people that I was unfamiliar with. We experienced racism there. I was very timid. Until I was thirty years old, I was unable to express myself. For a long time, I was ashamed to be an Indian. At school they told us that we were savages – that we burned and scalped missionaries. I didn't want anything to do with the terrible God of the Catholics, a punishing God who was willing to send us to hell. The only thing I wanted was truth. I wanted to know my Creator; I wanted to understand why we are here. I read the Bible.

I had a very low self-esteem because I had been abused by the priest. The priest would say to me in the confessional, "Come here, come closer, I can't hear you." And then he would touch me. Whenever the children came out of the confessional crying, I knew what was going on. For me, everything related to sex repulsed me. And I felt guilty, I was ashamed of it. I felt dirty. I understand those who were subjected to the same types of things.

When I was thirty years old, I wanted to know who I was. When I returned to Pikogan in 1980, I really started getting interested in what was happening to us collectively. The parents were drinking. I started becoming interested in my community. We are a people, not just people who drink. The Chief and I started working on raising awareness; we worked on personal development as well as establishing who we are as a people, not only as individuals. That was when I also started asking myself questions. The path that opened up to me was spirituality, my Creator. I established a relationship in my heart. That was how I started moving forward. Our soul and our spirit is what makes us human-beings. Little by little, others also started asking themselves important questions.

I relapsed during the 1990s for four years. I underwent therapy for fourteen months. I wanted to understand why I was the way that I was and that's when the residential school resurfaced, the passage of my being towards suffering. When I arrived at therapy, a person came to welcome me and it felt like the mother superior was coming to get me. They searched me and they searched my luggage and I felt like I was ten years old; I felt like a child even though I was forty-six years old. Afterwards, all I wanted was to get out of there. For fourteen months, it was like I was living at the residential school all over again. I worked on myself and that was when my second personal growth process began.

Today, people want to know even more about themselves. It is true that the more we talk about ourselves, the more we come out of our shell. We are then no longer the victim, we are free. The healing project, the path of healing – these are things I'm working on with my daughter. We held several support and therapy groups for former residential school students. Almost all of those who went to the residential schools have gone through them. The support group is intended for those who have parents who went to residential schools. This year we held a twelve-step program group. Those who participate in the group work together help each other and are only looking to resolve their issues. They wish to continue to progress. It's a project of the Healing Foundation. At first, the project was called "parenting skills", and then we looked to give it an Algonquin appellation and finally we named it "the path of healing", in order to help the families, all of the members of all of the families, in their healing processes.

Today, we have a nice community. I want the generations that didn't experience the residential schools to know the history of the communities so that they can understand why there are so many addictions issues. The history of Canada should be rewritten and then taught in schools. It's not only the residential schools that destroyed our populations. When the first missionaries arrived, that's when everything started. We couldn't touch the servants of God who taught us about hell and mortal sin. My parents never taught me religion. My grandfather was a faithful Catholic and it is true when people say that they wouldn't believe us when we told them that we were being abused. My family would spend ten months in the forest and then two months at Abitibi Lake. The priest came to preach every day. Beyond that, we didn't have religion. I don't believe in religion – it was man who invented religion, not God.

For the future, I want the First Nations to stand up and be recognized as a people; I want us to be recognized for what we went through and I want us to live in harmony with all other peoples. I want the children in the community to become reacquainted with their language, for everyone to be aware of what we are in the process of losing, of the importance of what we are losing. Our language is our identity. If you're an Algonquin, speak to me in Algonquin. My grandson has recently understood this.

I am proud of my grandchildren, they have assumed their responsibilities. When their parents so desired, I would welcome them in my home and let them stay with me. I wanted them to know where they were from. They had seen bad things, they didn't want their children to be subjected to the same things and so they left the community. I have a grandson who sings – his name is Samiens. He had started by writing poetry until eventually his sister asked him, "Why don't you sing?" and that's how his career started. He is interested in the history of the Indian residential schools; he talks about it clearly and openly. He denounces the injustices and requests recognition for his people. He often talks about me.

Photo: Patrice Gosselin

Photo: Patrice Gosselin

"It allowed me to live like my ancestors lived, one day at a time, getting the things that are needed and surviving. I was able to hold on to that, which allowed me to move forward, and reconnect with the values from my childhood."

Simon

Lac Simon, Saint-Marc-de-Figuery residential school

Our story is a never-ending story; we don't know where it truly begins. The process had already started before we even left for the residential schools. Our Elders would tell us about things that had happened well before we went to the residential schools. Sometimes, I tell myself that the residential school saved me. We lived in genuine poverty and social assistance programs didn't exist. We had to go hunting in order to survive or dig through the trash in lumber camps. I remember going through a week without eating – surviving by just drinking water. Our parents were really afraid of the government, of the white man. When my father killed a partridge or a hare, he told us not to tell anybody. The residential school saved me from that fate. I entered the residential school at the age of seven years and when I got out four years later, reality hit me. I knew what was waiting for us. Social programs didn't exist back then. They also often told me, "You can't let them take pictures of you" and I would wonder why.

As I was leaving the residential school, I knew that I was losing a lot of friends – all of the friends that I played sports with. We learned how to read. There was also religion – at one point I wanted to become a priest and I served mass whenever I could. That's where I experienced my first taste of wine.

I still ask myself a lot of questions to this day. I always felt that religion was collaborating with the government but I couldn't debate this point with the Elders. From a very young age I was politically involved in the community, at first just for the title, but eventually I made progress, I stopped using drugs and alcohol and started seeing the impacts and challenges and I started understanding. To this day, I ask myself if the communities are a good thing with the things that are going on inside of them; the answer isn't obvious when you look at how the people are doing. I traced my family tree; I'm related to everyone in the community at some point. Once you enter public life, you no longer have a private life and your past comes back to haunt you, even after twenty years.

Sometimes I ask myself if those who went to the residential schools use it as an excuse to keep using drugs and alcohol.

Today I know that I was fortunate to remain in contact with my grandfather; he is the one who enabled us to preserve our language. Each summer he brought us blueberry picking and told us stories and legends. Despite everything I went through at the residential school, I was able to keep my language, my culture – sometimes I tell myself that some of the best times of my life took place before the residential schools. We lived in different camps, and in the fall we would set off in a boat. I went to many camps. We had a camp at Lebel on *Quévillon*; we were a nomadic people. We would leave in the springtime and at Christmas; we made it up to Amos by travelling on the river. There wasn't any governmental pressure, we lived like free people. The residential schools changed me a lot; at the time my father was often at the hospital and sometimes we were alone with my mother. I lived pretty much everywhere; we often had to change camps. When I left the residential school, I returned to my community of Lac Simon. There wasn't much available there, no running water or electricity, we had to go outside even at night to answer the call of nature, even at minus forty degrees. We had to get water from the lake. My father was still a trapper and I had to take over for him when he went away. It should be mentioned that my parents were afraid of government authorities to the point of being afraid of hunting on our lands. From the age of 14 years, I used drugs and alcohol until I turned thirty years old. I got married when I was eighteen years old and my father-in-law would tell me to make things right. I had children. I didn't know anything about responsibility; I followed the same pattern as the one I experienced. My ex-wife shouldered all the responsibilities. When I quit drugs and drinking, it was because I no longer had a choice.

Then, I was elected chief and I wanted to save the community. This was back when the communities were given more control - Indian Affairs was transferring powers to the communities. I participated in discussions on the transfer process – I wanted to save my Nation but I forgot to save Simon.

I often wonder if I only wanted to be chief so I could fight and solve the hunting disputes; we weren't allowed to do anything back in those years, and so we started reclaiming our hunting and fishing rights. We also started asking ourselves why we had been placed in these communities. The residential school allowed me to speak with people from outside the community but it didn't succeed in taking from me what I had inside: my Aboriginal soul and my language.

Each person must come to the realization that we do not need to harm ourselves anymore in order to have a good life.

Today, we are losing a bit more of our language and we write more in French. We don't go into the forest anymore - I can no longer identity things in nature. One of the biggest problems we discover the further along we get in our healing process is the thing that is eating us up inside - our emotional dependency. We lost a lot from being removed from our parents. Our parents could never tell us they loved us; the parent-child bond is important. We must tell our children that we love them – our parents were there but they didn't say anything. My parents didn't go to the residential school. Today, I could talk about the things I went through with my children, as well as what they were going through when they started having their own problems. They indicated clearly to me that they had never had a father. They tell me, "We didn't have a father, we had a chief." My eldest is thirty-five years old, I am now a grandfather. I went to AA meetings for many years and they helped me to understand. I loved the movement because it allowed me to live like my ancestors lived, one day at a time, getting the things that are needed and surviving. I was able to hold on to that, which allowed me to move forward, and reconnect with the values from my childhood.

One day, I should write my autobiography in order to leave my community with all of the work and obstacles that must be overcome. Oftentimes, I tell myself that my thoughts are too far ahead for those in the community – we only become important and recognized once we are in our graves. In my personal reflections, like mourning a death, this should be a family issue. It isn't a community affair. We must make progress in that area. That's the way things once were, but things have changed.

I am proud of being a First Nations person, of having returned to my roots, of still being able to speak my language. In my opinion, language is an individual's identity. We must return to our roots in order to understand things and relearn our language in order to be able to transmit the rest, to reconnect with our culture, return to development in the way in which we had already started. We once did many things together, we must take our children camping again, do things together, travel with our children, like we did in the past – we would empty the community and go camping for a week, even two weeks at a time. Our youth should be asking for this. Even they are lost in the administrative jungle. If they really wanted to, everyone could go into the forest tomorrow morning.

Photo: Patrice Gosselin

"What I retained from the residential school that helps me today is my strength of character, autonomy, determination and my go-getter attitude."

William
Saint-Marc-de-Figuery residential school

I come from Rapid Seven. We moved here in 1970. We live on the first street that existed in Lac Simon and our house is either the first or second house to be built here in the community. Before I even went to the residential school, it was a source of pain. Whenever my brothers left, I would miss them a lot; it already had negative effects on me. I am the fourth of six children and my older brothers always left for the residential school. When I think about the residential school, it's always the smell that comes back to me, I haven't forgotten it. I can't describe the smell but I don't like it when it comes back to me.

Let me tell you about what I experienced - I experienced all kinds of things such as all sorts of abuse and lots of violence. Nonetheless, there were some good times. I played hockey in the beginning, I stayed at the residential school for two years and then I went to Lévicourt. At school, things went rather well at the elementary school level as well as for grades seven and eight, I was passing but I think my problems began near the end. After grade seven, I was unsuccessful, something was bothering me and that's when I started therapy. Even though I was a decent student at first, I could understand French, all of a sudden, I had a block. I couldn't write anymore, I was completely blocked, I couldn't even write simple sentences. Today, it's getting much better, even verbally-speaking, ever since I started progressing. Before, I had problems speaking, particularly in interviews, I am surprised to be here actually talking to you today.

After the residential school I had alcohol and drug abuse issues. I had my first child at seventeen years old, I started young, and then I had another daughter. My wife must have also gone to the residential school. We never talked about it. She passed away in 1990, but I believe that she went there as well. As for the parenting role, I thought that it had gone rather well for me. I did cause a lot of harm to my children because of addictions issues; I didn't even know why I was using alcohol and drugs. In 1990, I lost my wife in an accident. I was angry with the system; I had a lot of anger inside. In 1998, I had my first therapy; I had talked about going to therapy for a long time but I wasn't actually taking any steps.

After my first therapy, I thought that I had solved all my problems, but shortly afterwards I started having addictions issues again until 2005, when I had another therapy and then I resisted for another three or four months.

Finally, I went to another therapy session in June 2009, and this time it was really a great experience. I believe the difference was that this time during the therapy someone took me in their arms and held me - it really affected me and I cried. I was the first in the group to be held in someone's arms – the first to experience it; it was something so profoundly emotional. I like feeling the way that I do now. I don't want to forget the way I felt then or the way I felt while I was using; I mustn't forget or waste the sensation that I experienced. I know there are times when I relive similar experiences. Today, I am experiencing good feelings that I have never felt before.

I had stopped playing sports. Just being able to start playing hockey again, to relive the experience and feel the adrenaline pumping again was great. We'd tell ourselves that it was great, even if we lost; it was just great to be playing. We went to a hockey tournament one weekend. After we won the final game, someone took off with the cash reward. It didn't really bother me, it was just great to win. There is something that's even more important to me and that's taking care of myself. I do this by going fishing and participating in pow-wows and other activities that stimulate me. I don't neglect myself anymore; I have fun without drinking or using drugs. Before, in order to enjoy myself, I had to consume. I was sick and tired of staying home and drinking and using drugs.

I have worked for the department for the past sixteen years. For the last twelve years, I have been the general director of economic development. They kept me around for all those years; they must appreciate me after all. Nowadays, I work seventy hour weeks. Before, I missed a lot of work hours. Now, I like accumulating overtime hours. I enjoy my work, but it's difficult. Currently, we are looking to motivate the youth with projects that will be coming shortly, and give hope to the community in terms of the future of our youth. We have been working on this corporation structuring planning project for three years. This year is the implementation stage. The timing is great, I'm sober, if not I wouldn't be able to handle it. Before, if I was having a hard time, I would start using; if I scored a point, I'd go drink or use drugs to celebrate. There was always a good reason to be found. Is there a connection between my problems and the residential school? I denied it in the past, I couldn't even think about it for years. In 1998, I became aware of my issues. I truly worked a lot on myself, but I didn't do enough. There was still much work to be done. I believe that this time, I'm going to succeed.

Having a happy childhood means having the love and protection of our parents and being respected. My mother gave me enough love but I believe that I missed my father.

Whenever my brothers left for the residential school, they would disappear for several months at a time and I didn't know where they went off to. However, in addition to the separation, the thing I found the hardest to deal with was after three or four years our mother would say to us, "I don't recognize you anymore." There was a deep and genuine rupture – between us and within us.

An event triggered in me the will to live to the fullest. One day, I was hospitalized. There was a man in the bed next to mine in a terminal phase who was yelling, "I want to live, I want to live!" The man refused to die and that was a wake-up call for me. It was from that point on and increasingly so during the subsequent months, that I realized the importance of what I had heard. This person wanted to live, while I, with my alcohol and drug abuse, was killing myself. It had been my addictions that led me to the hospital in the first place.

I have always had good communication with my daughter, but with my son, it's an entirely different situation. We talk to each other but there is very little affection. They are resentful of me, they have not forgiven me yet, I talked to them a little bit about the residential schools; I discussed the issue a little but not more than that. It's important just to let them know where it all comes from.

Being a First Nations member means being proud of whom you are. I did neglect what I am, what I was. Today, I participate in pow-wows and ceremonies. I want this for myself and I also want to get my family to understand the direction I want to go to return to my roots. Today, my children have practically forgotten their language. They are still young and they can still change their mind. At that age, I also barely spoke my language, I had neglected it. It had become less important to me than drinking or using drugs.

What I retained from the residential school that helps me today is my strength of character, autonomy, determination and my go-getter attitude. I keep charging on even with the government. Even if there are roadblocks, I keep trying and trying and trying… we may even perhaps reach a global agreement. We've been negotiating it for two years, and I haven't given up.

As for the next generations, for the future, I wish them change. I asked a spiritual guide if I would see change in my community, and he told me that I would. That's what I want. We can start by developing businesses and creating jobs.

I would like to leave a legacy. I would like the members of my community to be proud of who they are. I want to develop projects so that they can find themselves, reconnect with their pride, and their freedom. To that end, I will keep pushing, for as long as I am able.

At the spiritual level, I am with the AA brotherhood and I've been involved in this group ever since I came out of therapy. I like participating in the conferences and I read a lot. I get involved in projects and play sports.

"Today, I am studying at the university and it's helping me a lot. When I left for the residential school I was five-and-a-half years old. Each time I leave for the university, I look at my children and it reminds me of when I left for the residential school. For me, all departures are the same departure, the same abandonment."

Edward

My name is Edward Shilton and I'm from the Atikamekw community of Wemotaci. I became aware that I needed to change my life when I got married and had my children. I was dealing with a lot of issues related to drugs and alcohol – particularly alcohol. There was always something that would lead me back to using. I felt something inside me that was choking me. I started understanding that what I had gone through at the residential schools was disrupting my life as a father of a family. I saw my children and I wondered why I was harming them. I understood that I had to free myself from a burden I was keeping inside of me. However, I still have that burden. It is still difficult for me, I always find it difficult. Each time I talk about it, it's as if I've returned to the residential school and I don't want to go back there. My wife and I, we talk, we try to help each other out but it's like we're turning in circles. There's no way out.

Currently, there is a lot of talk of healing and I know that I will not be able to heal. I am simply trying to mend my wounds. What I experienced is much too hard, it's too difficult. I want to be free of the burden, but I cannot remove what has been planted in my head. I have met with psychologists and therapists and they all tell me that I shouldn't be ashamed of what happened to me at the residential schools. But I only genuinely talk about the things that happened with my wife, and even to her, I don't say everything. It's shameful to me and the shame is unbearable. There is terrible anger inside of me because of what I was subjected to. It's what made us so violent later on, both my wife and I. Often, we say to each other, "Let's bury what happened to us." However, even if you do bury something, it always crawls back out. Plant a seed, and a tree will grow. If the seed is good, the tree shall be as well. If I bury something bad, what will come out then? I have returned to the places in which my experiences happened and I was just completely blocked, unable to react – just like the boy I once was. I could see myself; I could see little Edward being abused by the priest.

Today, there is not much out there that could make me happy. When I see my children, my grandchildren, I am happy, because I know that they will never be subjected to what I went through and that fills me with hope. I believe that this is the wish of all former residential school students who went through hell on earth, regardless of their race. Now, when people talk to me about religion, I have my doubts, I'm very sceptical. I remember quite clearly that the priest did the complete opposite of what the good sister who taught me asked me to do. Moreover, my parents were completely indoctrinated by the priest in the community and so it was pointless to blow the whistle, and so I kept everything to myself.

People today need to see it to believe it and it all took place at least fifty years ago. People are unable to believe things that happened so long ago, but for the former residential school students, the wounds haven't completely closed and they are so easily reopened.

Talking about it here does provide some relief but this type of relief it doesn't last long at all. It is coming out now, I feel a sense of liberation, but I fear its return. If I hadn't had children, I wouldn't be here today to talk about it. I want to stay in order to protect my children. I teach them about my spirituality because I lost faith in the Catholic Church. Those people do the opposite of what they say – and their so-called good Lord. Good? If their God is so good, why are we where we're at today? The meaning of good no longer holds value for me. In the spirituality that I share with my children, we talk to our Creator. I know that there is a greater being that can do whatever He wishes with me. There are still certain elements of the Catholic religion that I respect such as, for example, forgiveness, and reconciliation. Some people are able to forgive while others will never be able to forgive. They say that some acts are unforgivable and it's true. The violence that I subjected my wife to is unforgivable. And she tells me that she will not be able to forgive me. I understand her because I am also dealing with this inability to forgive.

Over the next ten years, my wish is for unity and mutual aid within my family followed by unity and mutual aid for the entire community. Look at our children, they are following in our footsteps and this is the heritage that we're leaving them with. I am a great-grandfather. Aboriginal people learn by observing and then doing.

It will take seven generations for the effects to disappear. We have been branded with a branding iron. It's in the past, but it isn't history. It's what our lives will have been about.

It is difficult being a First Nations member. Today, I am studying at the university and it helps me a lot. When I left for the residential school I was five-and-a-half years old. Each time I leave for the university, I look at my children and it reminds me of my departure for the residential school. For me, all departures are the same departure, the same abandonment. At the university, the youth don't know what to make of me. I sometimes wonder if something is written on my forehead. Have they heard something about my past? I feel like telling them, "Before judging someone, look inside yourself rather than in a mirror, for a mirror is just a reflection, a cover. You can do whatever you want with a cover but not with what's inside of you."

I am still not at peace with my life; I am not healed. I haven't made it to that stage yet. We can't change steps simply because we want to. In my adolescence, because of sports, it's as if I had a period of respite and that I had succeeded in setting aside my pain. Hockey helped me put it to rest. Then, I stopped playing sports and I started using drugs and alcohol. I hadn't forgotten what I had gone through after all, it was waiting for me. The same applies to all those who went to the residential schools. In a way, it's good that we don't forget so that it doesn't happen again. It should provide a reminder much like a tombstone. We must learn from past mistakes but it is also important to get through it.

When I was at the residential school, we were always quarrelling with the young Montagnais from Pointe Bleue. We fought behind the residential school; however we eventually became real friends. To this very day, we do various activities together. This was the only positive aspect of the residential schools. It created a very strong connection between us and we always talk about what happened to us. I'm not sure at what point we became aware that it was wrong for us to hate each other, to despise each other so much. Now, the Atikamekws and the Innus from Mashteuiatsh have become the greatest friends in the world. All Aboriginal people love sports. We played a lot with the Hurons as well and developed connections with them. We shared with the other Nations our history in the residential schools.

In my opinion, it would be in our best interests to listen to each other. If we recount everything that happened, it mustn't just become a storybook because it's very real. Reality must not be denied. The thing that bothers me the most is the compensation they gave us. It's as if they're buying off our silence and our disappearance. "Here you go Edward, now go back to your reserve." I wish the government would show us what they are hiding from us. Maybe it would help us to understand. Today, an adult who looks at children in a school yard is immediately thrown in jail. So why did the government entrust us to abusers? If we could understand that, perhaps we could heal. The way things stand now, it's only the former residential school students who are becoming transparent. This story must not be used to cause harm or destroy. It must serve to clarify events and to teach those who are not aware of what happened. It is always frightening to talk about it and show your emotions but it always provides a little bit of relief.

I would like to see a commemorative plaque in each community like for the holocaust in Germany, to ensure that it doesn't ever happen again and so that we can remind ourselves of what must be avoided. Also, the history of the residential schools must be completely integrated into the Canadian history books. It also shouldn't be called the history of Canada. Canada wasn't discovered because it already existed. This country should be given a name that identifies it as an Indian land. Then perhaps we can talk about healing and reconciliation.

"One day, someone came into my office and wept in my arms, and I was able to help that person go on living."

Espérance
Matimekush-Lac John

I come from Matimekosh Lac John and I attended the Indian residential school in Maliotenam from 1964 to 1968. I went to school in Schefferville until the third grade. The teacher was a priest, and we were all taught together in the same room. Then, they started sending us into town, to Notre-Dame, and that's where I spent my fourth grade. The following year, my mother went to see the priest in order to send me to the residential school.

I never had the opportunity to discuss it with them but I was upset with my parents for sending me there for a long time. My father already worked for a company. We were thirteen children and we all went to the residential school one after the other – some of us were there at the same time. When it was my turn to go, I didn't understand why I was going there. There were many of us and all I remember is that I was crying and couldn't recognize anyone. I remember feeling like I was being locked in. The nuns were tired of hearing me because I was always crying. When I think back, I feel a sense of imprisonment. In my memories, I can't see where I am, but I'm all alone and I can't stop crying.

In the beginning, I was in the group of young children. There were nuns, brothers and sisters who took care of us. I was young but even then I could tell that strange things were going on. I remember a brother who worked there; he would take the little girls and walk around with them. I was afraid of him and didn't trust him. Then, when I went with the older children, I saw what he was up to. Each time he entered the large hall, he would run after us and pretend to tickle us but he was actually touching us. At first, I thought that he wanted to play, but one time, everyone had gotten away and he cornered me and my friend in the locker room. She held on to me tightly so that I wouldn't leave her alone and he touched us everywhere. I managed to run away and went to tell the others to come and save my friend. The others came and he laughed at us as he left. I thought that he wanted to have fun with us but later I understood that he we was actually doing something else. He had bad intentions and now I know why I was so uncomfortable around him.

We didn't talk about it to each other. It was only once we started talking openly about the residential schools that I really found out everything that had happened. Everything I heard about the sexual abuse that happened there, I heard it during the first symposium that took place in Sept-Îles. That was when I found out what had happened to the others – that others had experienced horrible things and I had been relatively lucky. I often think about the little girls who were there with me. The brother was always with them; he would hold them up and have them sit on him.

There were times that were bad but also times that were happy. Sometimes we all came together and got to see my brothers and sisters. I had an older brother and a younger brother at the school at the same time as me. We were not allowed to visit the boys' side. Sometimes we saw them in the dining hall and they could see us as well; they kept an eye on us to try to protect us as best they could. Eventually, because we spoke so much French, when we returned home for the Holidays, we couldn't speak our language anymore. They really isolated us from each other.

After the residential school, I went to school in the town of Sept-Îles. This is where we started being subjected to punishment. We would escape on weekends and the last time we did this, when we got in, the nun was waiting for us and she sent us to the dormitory without any dinner. For an entire month, we had to go to bed at 6:30 pm even though the weather was nice – it was the month of September. Another time we were beaten because there had been a theft in the priests' dining quarters. We had made off with soda, fruit – all types of things that we weren't allowed to have. There was a canteen but none of us had any money. In the spring, the nuns found the empty bottles that we had left outside. When they interrogated us one by one, they asked us "How many bottles did you steal? We know it was you, how many did you steal?"

And then, at one point, we started defending ourselves. At around fourteen or fifteen years of age, we went to Sept-Îles by bus and we didn't go back. We strolled around and visited Innu families in Uashat. We knew that we would be punished when we returned but we also knew that we could defend ourselves. I was expelled. I had been running away all the time anyway. At that point I went into a foster family.

I returned to Malio and dropped out of school. We started drinking – we were free, many of us together, and then we started having problems. My addictions issues lasted for a long time, even after my marriage with my spouse. My three children were subjected to family violence. It was when we underwent therapy with the Healing Foundation that I understood the root of my problems.

Before, we never really talked about things, we only talked about our mischievous acts and we laughed about them. We never discussed what had really happened. I underwent therapy for five years and it helped me a lot. Before I would ask my children to help me with household chores and I was never satisfied. They would make the beds or do the dishes but I would redo everything, I was never happy. My relationships with my children were always difficult. I treated them exactly the way I was treated at the residential school. To this day, I sometimes fall back into the habit and I have to be careful because my children let me know.

In 1975, I already had two children but I wanted to work – to regain control over myself. I started working as a receptionist at the band council; I replaced my friend who wanted to become a teacher. I worked for the band council for thirty years.

I retired in 2005. I spent time travelling and went on trips. I like meeting people but I'm not the type of person who approaches others; I leave that to those who are with me and I let them express themselves. We already had a group and I was familiar with the story of the survivors. I decided to get involved with the Healing Foundation.

None of the parents had spoken about the residential school experience with their children and many of their children didn't even realize that their parents were former residential school students. I sent the children of former residential school students into the forest with a psychologist. My son also went with his girlfriend. His girlfriend's father is also a survivor. Both of them wished to learn more about what happened to their parents – and that's where everything really started. I've been progressing ever since. Today, I'm doing well.

The things I do today, such as helping others and crying with them, really affect me and help me. One day, someone came into my office and wept in my arms, and I was able to help that person go on living. I was there for him. So I didn't cry with him, I had the strength to care for him. Sometimes though I'm unable to hold it in and it feels good just to let it out.

To recharge my energy, I pray. I did not set my religion aside, despite the residential school. I learned to pray in a small chapel and I continue to work at the church with the priest. Back in the day, I was unable to discuss the residential school with him, and then one day, I announced to him that I was working with the residential school survivors. He told me that it was good, that he knew that I could help them. He told me that during meetings he also discussed what had happened with his colleagues. I was worried that he would be angry with me because we discussed what certain priests had done, but he was very understanding. There are some elders who want nothing to do with the church because they don't like the religion they were subjected to in the residential schools. Regardless, religion is still important to me and nobody can stop me from practicing it. Not all priests are out to hurt people. I believe that reconciliation, a path to healing, cannot happen if the priest and nuns aren't involved.

Things are going well today in my family. Our problems used to be caused by drinking. I stopped drinking. I have nine grandchildren, one of which is a 19 year old who still lives with me – he has always lived with me. For the past four months he has been working. Today, it is my children who are starting to become aware of the example they are providing to their children. They are always watching them closely. Every night, they keep an eye on things to see what they are up to, where and they are and who they are with. My husband and I used to do the same thing. So, I tell them, "Now, it's your turn."

Today, I am not healed but I'm on the right path. I love what I'm doing with my group. There are still people who are too shy to talk about their experiences. Some people are considering it but aren't quite ready yet. We started going into the forest with the Foundation along with psychologists and interveners. We went with our children and now we want to bring our grandchildren.

I hope the youth will come with us into the forest because I know they want to come; there are some who ask if they can come along on weekends. I organized a group of young Innu dancers that is composed of five girls and five boys. When I was looking for people to show them how to dance, a male teacher for the boys and a woman for the girls, neither of them asked for money. We had the opportunity to travel. We wanted to go to France in 2011, but they only wanted 11 year olds. Mine are older and I don't want to let them down. Today, however, I need money for the regalia and I'm waiting for caribou skins.

Photo: Pascal Plamondon-Gomez

Collection of life stories of the survivors of the Quebec Indian Residential Schools

Photo: Hemera

Sometimes still at night, I sit in from of my house, I turn off the lights early in order to be able to think more clearly. I stare into the darkness. I stay alone in the dark to recharge my batteries and I tell myself, "Tonight I'm happy because I didn't take anything, we'll worry about tomorrow when it comes."

François

My name is François Basile. I am the eldest of seven children. I have two brothers and five sisters, one of whom passed away at the residential school from a cancerous tumour in 1969. I am from Wemotaci but I was born at the hospital in La Tuque – that is what my mother told me. I went to the Saint-Marc-de-Figuery residential school in Amos for two years and then I went to Pointe Bleue for nine years, which today is called Mashteuiatsh.

I was hesitant to tell my story today, but I know now that people must know that happened. They must hear the residential school story and learn about the children we once were. Ever since I was thirteen years old I had to support a family. Everything I earned, I gave it to my mother so that we could have enough to eat. I didn't earn a lot of money but it was enough to cover the family's basic needs. I performed summer jobs such as wood cutting. Then, I got married, and eventually I got divorced. I had six children; the eldest suffered an accidental death in 1999. I have five daughters left. I am a grandfather as well as a great-grandfather; I have thirteen grandchildren in total.

As for my attendance at the Indian residential schools, I was well treated in Amos. As for Pointe-Bleue, I was abused by a priest when I was an adolescent. After spending nine years there, I ran away. In fact, there were four of us who ran away; we could no longer deal with the type of treatment we were being subjected to. That was when I quit school, but I later returned because it was something I really needed. The residential schools were not all bad; there was also some good to be found there – not in the way we were treated, but the things we were taught. The things we learned we still use to this day. The hardest part for me was what I was subjected to. It's what led me to drug and alcohol abuse.

When I finally ran away from the residential school at the age of fourteen years, I had been abused since the age of twelve. My grandparents were the ones who cared for me, and so I tried to discuss it with them. I told my grandfather what had happened but he didn't believe me. I took advantage of any opportunities I could find to talk about it but he wouldn't listen to me. He believed the priests. I started abusing drugs and alcohol at the age of twelve years – especially alcohol. I also experimented with drugs but they weren't really for me. When I went through the hearing process, it was very hard on me. I went as far as I could but I couldn't go all the way – I couldn't relive the whole experience. It will always stay with me. My children and grandchildren don't ask me too many questions. Moreover, up to a certain age, communication was difficult. Even after three therapies, I was unable to talk about everything; I am still carrying a burden within me. Today, I do the best I can, but many things remain unresolved.

My last therapy was in 2003. I have still yet to achieve sobriety and it's a back and forth battle. Now, I have moderated my consumption. When I relapse, I have a difficult time accepting what I'm doing. I'm not proud of myself. When my spouse left, I felt like I was in a black hole. Since I wasn't present at the time, she believed that I was in agreement with the divorce. Afterwards, I attempted suicide twice. Today, I am happy to have the opportunity to know my grandchildren. They are here for a reason. I didn't get to see my children grow up because of my drinking.

The thing that helped me change the most is communication. From the moment I started opening myself up, a spark of hope was rekindled. Communication is coming to me more easily now. During the hearing, I had to stop because I found it too difficult. Then, I talked about it with my young ones. They must go to school outside the community; they will never know the residential school. However, the isolation remains difficult. They tell me that the best therapy is to talk about what happened, and it's true. Now, from time to time, I do feel better. What also helps me is spending time with others who have struggled with drug and alcohol issues. When I return home, I think about what we experienced at the residential schools. When I listen to others, I can see that our stories are similar.

I built myself a cabin in the forest on the outskirts of the community on my father's hunting land. It would make me so happy to be able to build my home on my ancestral lands and live in a place without drug or alcohol consumption. When people who drink or use drugs come, I take off in my vehicle. When my daughters visit me, we walk with the children and have a conversation with them in the Atikamekw language. The forest offers me respite and sets me on the correct path. And yet, the bad returns to me all too often.

What makes a happy childhood is continuous communication while avoiding problems for our children. My daughters quit school early and they would like to return. I abandoned them and it's difficult for both them and me. Living off of social assistance is far from the ideal situation. I visit my daughters at their homes. I always spent more time drinking than working. I spent my salary on my addiction. There was always much more alcohol at home than clothing or food. I really hope that they don't live their lives the way did. I don't know if they will ever forgive me.

I don't want the new generations to travel the same path that I did. I want them to travel their own path; I want them to be happy. My life was miserable. My father left when I was very young and our mother was authoritative. I used drugs and alcohol to forget what was happening to me, I drank and when I woke up, things were even harder than before. Today, I have to overcome my addictions, escape the vice, and once I succeed, I must develop a healthy lifestyle. I want my children to provide my grandchildren with nothing but good things. Being a great-grandfather is my greatest source of pride today.

I'm a generous person. With my indemnities, I helped those close to me pay off their debts, I bought a sewing machine for the mother of my children – we have a good friendship. I have a tendency to prioritize others, particularly my family first, followed by friends and peers. I have always taken care of others since I was a boy; I want to have good communication with those who are close to me. I don't really know what I really want to be, I only know that I would like to be at peace with myself and everything I experienced. I try to forgive; forgiveness is within reach but I'm unable to forget, that's a whole different story. Sometimes still at night, I sit in from of my house, I turn off the lights early in order to be able to think more clearly. I stare into the darkness. I stay alone in the dark to recharge my batteries and I tell myself, "Tonight I'm happy because I didn't take anything, we'll worry about tomorrow when it comes." Sometimes, I manage to make it through a good stretch without drinking. I try to stay with positive people, to live in the present, to avoid looking back and instead think about tomorrow. These things work for me. I wish I could always conduct myself appropriately and have positive relationships with people. When someone says something negative to me, it affects me for a long time. I'll spend two or three days without speaking and walk along the river, feeling ashamed. I don't want to harm anyone and I always feel unimportant.

I went to Domrémy and I did a lot of work on myself. And then I gave up trying. I put my tools away. I should take them back out. I don't know if my testimony will help you at all. I've heard testimonies in the past and I remember telling myself, "That's me, that's my story, that's my life." I wish I could have had a different life, a different path. At one point, I became confused, things became too difficult and I felt sorry for myself. The important thing is to hear the stories of the survivors and understand the connection between childhood, the residential schools and the road we had to travel.

We must acknowledge our qualities and our courage, and recognize ourselves and each other.

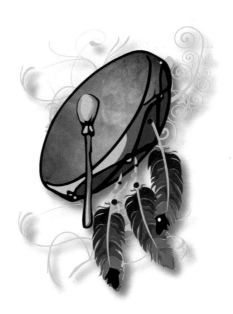

"Life is a mystery that I resolved with my heart because I wanted to change. I don't ask for pity from people when I talk about my past; rather what I want is to explain to them how I pitied myself and all the pain I was carrying around with me."

Jimmy

We were three brothers at the La Tuque residential school. We were very young at the time and I didn't know what it meant back then. There was a cross at the entrance to the school. The day they came to get us, my parents didn't understand what was happening. They said, "We will take your children and they will go to a good school. They will become doctors, nurses or whatever they want. All you have to do is sign these papers." My father replied 'No, I won't allow my children to go." The RCMP officer and the social worker from our community told my father that he would go to prison if he didn't authorize them to do what they wanted. We were behind our parents near the bed, I remember quite well. It was a very emotional event for my parents and for us as well. They succeeded in removing us from our family. When we arrived at La Tuque, they brought us into a building with a cross at the entrance. Two boys from our community were there. They were wearing costumes. I knew those boys. My brother and I could hear them talking. I understood English because I had attended an Anglican school. They were saying that there was no more room for the two of us in the residential school because there were too many children. They were right because one of my brothers and I were brought to Montreal to a boarding school for boys administered by Catholics. That was where we spent the next six years.

I don't believe that we were the only ones to have been sent elsewhere. Other children left for boarding schools for boys. I've been thinking about it since this residential school issue has resurfaced. Many children were sent to other places. Am I entitled to compensation because I was sent elsewhere? They only wrote in our file that we were not recognized as former residential school students. One of my brothers told me that we had to go to court and we are thinking about it. We were supposed to go to the residential school however, because it was overcrowded, they sent us to a different place. What we went through was identical – it was the same thing.

I stayed there for almost seven years before returning home. It was difficult for us. The only thing we thought about was returning home. We would ask those in charge of the program "When will we be going back home?" Sometimes they would reply "Never." Just like at the residential school, we were forbidden to speak our language. We had to speak English at all times – nobody was allowed to speak their native language.

We talk about it with my brother - the one who stayed at the residential school. We experienced the same thing, the same program. He talks to us about physical abuse, much like the abuse we were subjected to at the boarding school for boys. It was exactly the same thing. They shaved our heads. When we spoke our language, they washed our mouths with soap. We were forced to whisper to each other. They repeatedly said to us that English was our native language; thankfully they didn't have that power. I heard children being struck. I can still hear their screams at night when I'm sleeping. We were so afraid at the boarding school for boys that we would push our beds together in case someone came. Oftentimes, an employee would enter the dormitory and hit us while we were sleeping. One of us had to stay awake in order to watch over the others. I believe that the history of the residential schools was the greatest crime committed against Aboriginal people.

I lost a lot in this story. If I had stayed with my father, he would have taught me the culture and traditions of our people. He would have taught me how to hunt. I lost all of that. My father also suffered a loss, since he was responsible for my care. From my standpoint, it's exactly as if the government had told my father that he was unable to take care of his child, of his home. The only thing I took from this experience is the violence, suffering and suicidal thoughts that lead me to using drugs and alcohol. It completely changed my life.

To this day, I have tried to recognize my traditions and culture to the best of my ability. My friends and I are First Nations members and I'm proud of that. I was able to preserve my language and I transmitted it to my two sons. A few years ago, social services tried to take my children from me. I had to fight in order to maintain custody. I told the court "I won't let what happened to me happen to my children." I had to explain to the Crown what I had experienced during all those years. We are American Indians. We aren't bothering anyone. All of this must stop. I've never tried to change anyone. When I look at myself I am proud of what I see. Now, my son is at home and he speaks our language very well. He has the long hair of an American Indian and that's how I want to see my child. I never had that opportunity when I was over there.

The boarding school for boys left me with many scars. I had to embark on a path of healing in order to find the solutions to break free. I took the necessary steps to appease my anger. I think that many of the boys who were subjected to the residential schools turned to drugs and alcohol when they returned to their communities. It allowed them to feel alright, because when you're sober, your memories return and your scars surface.

The most important thing I had to do was to make a decision on my own. When I realized for the first time that I was an alcoholic, it was a significant sense of awareness, a spiritual opening. I understood that I shouldn't be living this way, that it wasn't me! I had to make my own choices. I could have kept on blaming others for the rest of my life. As of today, I have been sober for 23 years. I exercise and I have a university certificate. I talk about my past in order to help others and to try to understand why all of this happened. My grandfather, who was a wise man, said to me one day "Everything that happens in life is about survival, whether good or bad." Even the Elder who taught me in Saskatchewan told me to balance the good with the bad to strike a balance in my life.

Who helped me the most in my life? I did! I was incarcerated because of my violence; I am not ashamed to say it. I hated being in prison. I promised myself that I would never go back. And I never did return. Life is a mystery that I resolved with my heart because I wanted to change. I don't ask for pity from people when I talk about my past; rather what I want is to explain to them how I pitied myself and all the pain I was carrying around with me.

My children go out with their friends. I know that they will be subjected to a lot of peer pressure. When they return home, we talk about it. The residential school shaped me as a father. There weren't only bad sides, because we did receive an education. We kept the education we received and it helped us in our lives.

I wear my American Indian identity with pride. We went to our cabin this weekend to go hunting. When we aren't working, we try to do activities with the children. They like new technologies and devote a lot of time to them. They go out with their friends. They need to experiment with their social lives.

The residential school was a very brutal experience for us. Those who worked there broke the law. It's unfair to let the priests who caused so much harm in our lives to get away with it unscathed. What would I like to see happen? I would like to bring out the genuine nature of the First Nations, our culture and our traditions. I would like to bring it all back and listen to the Elders tell us who we were, how we lived and then return to how we once lived. We would even like to hear about our tragedies before our Elders pass on. I only recently learned, three weeks ago in fact, where my brother was laid to rest in Northern Quebec. It was an Elder who provided me with this information because my father passed away. This is an example of what I was deprived from because of the residential schools. We have lost a part of our history and our knowledge because of the government. The women were forced to learn how to create moccasins and snowshoes all over again.

I heard a government representative apologize to us. I don't understand why it isn't those who are directly involved that come to tell us they are sorry for the treatment they subjected us to. We should bring the people who are guilty to an American Indian gathering, a gathering of healing. They would then understand the importance of apologizing to us. We would apply American Indian justice while sometimes talking to them about the Circle. We would decide what is to follow. It would be the starting point and this time it would be done correctly. We allow the East, West, North and South join in a great ceremony of healing.

"I work a lot at the school towards community healing in accordance with the four Anishnabe principles: sharing, respect, honesty and humility. I broke it all down into simple words so that the young people can understand the teachings of our parents."

Marie-Jeanne

I was born naturally, like back in the old days, in a tent in the forest. We lived like nomads in the forest. My grandfather had his house here; we'd meet up with him during the summer and then we were off trapping for the rest of the year. I was a very happy little girl. We got around with snowshoes and dogsleds.

And then, all of a sudden, everything changed. I didn't understand what was going on. There was a large grey bus that I had to get on. For a long time, I didn't understand where this bus was taking me or what I was going to do once I got there. Even when I got to the residential school, I still didn't understand. They said to us "Get in line, line up!" Since we didn't understand their language, they pulled on our arms. And so I experienced fear for the first time. With my family, I wasn't afraid of anything. My family took care of us and protected us from danger. At the residential school, it was a completely different situation. I spent my time crying. I tried to follow instructions and do like everyone else did in order to avoid punishment. When we didn't listen, they pulled our ears. I always had earaches. Today, I have an ear I can barely hear with. Before getting on that bus, I was a child who was loved and spoiled; we took turns staying at our grandparents place. After we returned from the residential school, our family started calling us white people because we could no longer understand them. We weren't allowed to speak our language over there, and if we did, we were punished and we had to do lines. The nuns would hurt me but I would defend myself, I would remove their headdress or just push them. We were five girls who were always together and we protected each other. Therefore, they left me alone.

I spent six years at the residential school. Then, I went to Senneterre for two years in an English language school and so once again I could no longer understand anything. I was in sixth grade and they sent me back down to third grade. I was really proud of myself at the residential school. I was really good at mathematics and fairly good at French. At Senneterre, at the English school, I experienced problems.

I couldn't understand English. I stayed there for three years until grade 7. Then, they sent me to Louvicourt and they put me back in grade 5. Once again, I lost all my self-esteem. However, I didn't give up; I continued up to grade 8. Finally, however, I was forced to stop because my mother became ill.

I resented my parents for having let me go. I had to leave so quickly without knowing what was going on. I didn't even know I was going to school. That was what sparked my anger. When we returned for the summer, my brother and I did things our own way. We rebelled and didn't listen anymore.

Then, I lived my own life, I got married young and I also got pregnant young. My parents didn't want anything to do with me once I got pregnant. My grandparents came to get me and they brought me to Senneterre. They had become Pentecostals and according to their movement, I had broken the rules because my child had been conceived before marriage. I left the house in order to move in with my husband. I lived with his family. My husband had spent his childhood with his kokom, his grandmother. She became my kokom. I learned a lot from her in the areas of culture, language and traditional recipes.

I had three children. It was always kokom who cared for them when we were drinking. Kokom passed away at 61 years of age. My mother's rejection was difficult for me, but thankfully my addictions weren't a major problem; I didn't like the taste of alcohol and tobacco. I used it to numb the pain. I always felt abandoned, whenever I made a mistake or when my ex left me. Did I deserve to be abandoned? I always ask myself this question. I started rebuilding a relationship with my mother not so long ago – now we go into the forest or town together.

Yes, we are always in need of others. At the residential school I learned French, reading and writing. When I thought about what I wanted to be when I grew up, I hesitated between becoming a teacher or a nurse. In the summertime at my parents' house, the nurse would arrive with her handbag and little white hat. I would go see her and I wanted to be like her – I wanted to be a nurse. Then later on when I went to the residential school I wanted to become a teacher. When I watched the teachers working I knew it would be something that I'd like to do. For a while, I changed my mind because of the hate I carried inside me. Then, later on, I returned to school in Chicoutimi where I completed my program. Afterwards I taught for thirteen or fourteen years at the elementary school level.

During that time, I was also a member of Council. When I was elected at the band council, I asked for training in order to do my job well and understand negotiation strategies. Today I am doing well and I enjoy what I do.

I don't talk about the residential school with my children; I simply tell them that they are very fortunate. What I went through belongs to me and I went to therapy in order to resolve it. I didn't even tell anyone when I left for therapy. I stayed there for three intensive weeks in order to work on myself. I had many dreams while I was there. It took me a long time to forgive. Every time I meet priests or nuns, I wonder why they subjected us to all of that if they really work for God.

Is it my calling to fight in order to prevent our children from being subjected to the same things? I don't like it when the social services place children. I became the school principal seven years ago and I always ask to see how the youth and students who have been placed are doing. It concerns me a lot. I don't want them to go without good food like we did at the residential school.

I work a lot at the school towards community healing in accordance with the four Anishnabe principles: sharing, respect, honesty and humility. I broke it all down into simple words so that the young people can understand the teachings of our parents. When a moose was killed, our parents would share the meat in order to ensure that everyone was fed.

At the school I work at, I implemented a teaching system that aims to get the children to go outdoors. For the past two years, they have slept in tents. A work colleague, who retired, said to me, "I'm going to learn everything that my mother can pass down to me." She has been learning from her mother the traditional teachings which she then passes on in the park. The children gather around her. These teachings are now a part of the school program.

I have three children and fourteen grandchildren who are extremely important to me. When my children were young, my parents would give me money in order help me send my children to hockey or broomball. I would accumulate debts each year in order to pay for their equipment and registrations for various tournaments. I wanted my children to be comfortable and have what I never had. I want my grandchildren to do the same as I did: go to school in order to get the tools and resources that they need to work for the community. I always worked for my children and for the community.

My wish is for the community members to heal from all of the suffering they have gone through. They have to learn how to be happy again as they once were. I started being happy at the residential school when I started to learn – I still love learning to this day. I want the youth in the community, including the young mothers and the young fathers, to return to school and then come back to work in the community for the well-being of everyone.

I spent my whole life working on myself. Marie-Jeanne, stop being afraid, stop suffering, get out of your shell and get out there and go get what you want. Our youth must get back on their feet and get in touch with the resource people who are still here in our community so that they can help them to become reacquainted with Anishnabe culture. These people want to help.

Photo: Hemera

"By that time, I could no longer speak my language; I couldn't even understand the children my age anymore. My brother had to translate what I was saying to my grandparents. I was forced to adapt to this new life, to family life."

Mary

To tell the truth, you are opening a forty-five year old wound. I believe I was the youngest residential school student in La Tuque; I was only eight years old at the time. We were promised a good education if we went to school. Our parents therefore signed the authorization papers and, in the month of August, we left for the residential school. We only returned home the following summer. That year, I didn't see my parents or grandparents again. It was very difficult. Upon arrival at the residential school, we lost our names; we were assigned numbers. I was no longer Mary but rather M3. In the girls section there were flowers and in the boys section there were animals. There were four sections for the girls and each section regrouped several communities. We all had a number on our clothing. They cut our long hair and told us that we had lice. I always wondered why I was the only person in my family who wore glasses. Later on, I remembered that when they were washing our hair with vinegar in order to kill the lice, I got some in my eye. As of the very next day, I was wearing glasses.

I nonetheless retained many memories of my childhood spent with those who are close to me. I remember going to school with my friends. It was a very small school. I still wonder today how come my brother and I were selected to go to the residential school. Was it because we were living with our grandparents?

I returned home two years later. People from our community had come to the residential school in order to see how we were being treated. They didn't like what they saw. I believe that at that point the band council no longer wanted us to return. By that time, I could no longer speak my language; I couldn't even understand the children my age anymore. My brother had to translate what I was saying to my grandparents. I was forced to adapt to this new life, to family life.

There weren't only bad things during those two years. I did learn English. I also learned to make my bed. But the thing that helped me the most is religion. My people are very religious.

There was always fighting between the residential school students. I had bruises everywhere. I never talked about it; I wanted to leave that in the past. Later on, when I started filling out the first forms in order to indicate how I was treated, I was only able to sign my name. It was too difficult to immerse myself in everything that had happened.

I wasn't raped or touched inappropriately. I wasn't subjected to this type of abuse. I was the youngest. I fought with those who pulled my hair. I suffered because of my eye – it was really painful.

In the beginning, we were all in the same large school. Then one day, they said that those who showed improvement in their grades would go to school downtown. I was chosen. It was a great advantage for me. I walked every day in order to go to school. Few among us had that opportunity. I was pleased to have the chance to escape those walls and it was difficult to return at the end of each afternoon. I didn't like their food. We always ate the same things every week and we never ate traditional food. We had to go to church every day before going to school. If I could start my life over again, I wouldn't go to the residential school. My children were not subjected to this experience and I don't want my grandchildren to go through it either.

Today, most of my children have left the house. I have only one left. He is twenty years old. Their father had an accident and he was left paralyzed. My children had to care for him. Since I am not strong enough to move him from his bed to his bath, I need the strength of their arms. I am still here. My reward is that my children love traditional food, speak their language and love to hunt.

Having a happy childhood means living under the same roof with one's mother and father. I never had that chance. I was raised by my grandparents. I cannot say that I had a happy childhood. My father passed away when I was young. My mother remarried and established another family.

I would like my community to become united. I see children, people from my generation as well as youth who know nothing about our traditions. It would be nice if they could just say "I will try." Try with all their heart. If you commit yourself to it, it'll be different. If you really want to learn something, you can. Sometimes, when it's difficult, people give up and turn towards drugs and alcohol. My brother died from that. He went to the residential school and I think his experience was worse than mine. He never spoke to me about it but he was very tormented by it. I never found out what was happening on the boys' side. We weren't allowed there. The only time I would see him was when we played outside. It was hard not to be able to talk to my own brother or sister. They separated us – they would never place family members together.

I am doing better now. To have made it through such a difficult life motivates me to continue being the person I am today. I could have used drugs and alcohol; I probably wouldn't be sitting here today. Sometimes, when my memories resurface, it is very painful. Especially when I look at my grandchildren who are the same age I was when I was forced to leave. I want my children and grandchildren to be happy and I want them to receive love and understanding. I want them to be proud of who they are. I hated the residential school so much that I hated myself as an Aboriginal person. It took many years of therapy for me to accept myself the way that I am.

Today, I am really proud of being an Aboriginal person. I would not change my identity. The problem I have now is that I can't find enough time to do everything that I'd like to do. I have a job as an advisor. I want to put time aside to go into the forest, to go fishing on a boat, to go for a truck ride; these are things I like to do. My children were raised in the forest.

My grandmother was a seamstress and I didn't have the chance to learn from her. There aren't any more women from my generation who know how to sew or clean a caribou today. We have lost all of that. It's great to have electricity and running water and to be able to benefit from new technologies, but you mustn't lose your soul. I had to learn my language all over again; people still laugh at my accent. I had lost my identity. I didn't respect myself anymore. I had to talk to other women, pray and undergo therapy; that is how I became stronger.

The thing that would make me the happiest would be having the opportunity to participate once again in the workshops that allowed us to talk about our past. I would have liked for these to continue - being able to gather with other survivors in a circle or in the forest was healthy. Many people, particularly men, keep everything inside. They are unable to reveal their sentiments and they don't want to discuss what happened to them. Many of the men who went there are dead. We would need a resource person to guide these workshops; someone who knows and understands us.

Photo: Hemera

"One day I was with my father. He was walking in front of me. I felt so proud and carefree; I finally felt like a complete person. In the forest, everything they said about me at the residential school just went away."

Taddy

My name is Taddy André. I was born in "The Place Where the Lake Moves Forward", in Labrador. I am a former student of the Maliotenam residential school. We were ten children in my family. When my brothers and sisters left, I cried. I was too young to follow them. Then, on the following month of September, my mother passed away. I spent ten years of my life at the residential school.

Before, we lived in a home that my father had purchased in Uashat. It is important to specify that because there are people my age who believe that the government has always been there for us and that everything has always been free. Before, to send a child to school, it was necessary to pay for the materials and the education in general. The parents supported their children. They would go into the forest for ten months in the year and, upon their return to Uashat, they could purchase their homes. We travelled on foot and by canoe.

My father was born in 1924 approximately ten kilometres from the place I was born. Everyone is proud of their place of birth because it is part of who we are. Yet, at the residential school, we were declared natives of Sept-Îles. Why didn't they respect our roots?

I remember a winter during which our tent burnt down. We always remember strong emotions that we experienced in the past. I always enjoyed going into the forest, climbing trees and going fishing. Back in those days, we weren't shut into the reservations. One day, our parents were forbidden from accessing their lands. They were risking incarceration if they broke the law. When my father tried to return to his lands, they stopped him. What would a white person do if he/she was forbidden to work and to feed his/her children? My father said "Even if I receive a house and some money, what do you want me to do with it?" But the decision had been made and the faster we were off the land, the sooner they could do whatever they wanted to do with it. That was when the damage started.

I went to the residential school like my brothers. Our father told us that it would be good for us. Life was after all quite difficult in the forest. As a child, I tried to do the best I could, to follow the rules and even think like the white people did. Of course, we did learn many things but we lost many things as well. They wanted us to believe that it was better this way. The consequences of these years spent at the residential school I understood later on. One day, in my community, I wanted to help the leisure committee. In this committee there was a priest, a white person and an Innu person. The Innu never spoke up except to say "Great Idea!" whenever the priest made a suggestion. It would have been better to get more involved and for us to take care of things. Our children were at stake. I didn't like the fact that the priest was deciding everything while the Innu person who was representing us wasn't speaking up. I understood then that we hadn't learned to be responsible for ourselves.

Sometimes, those who lived in Maliotenam could get out and go home. We had to stay at the residential school since we didn't have a family. We never received any affection; all human-beings require affection. The only thing we could do was try to get through it. I always wanted to learn and receive an education. I wanted my children to have the best of everything. We lost our ambition because of the residential school without even noticing it. These schools were under federal jurisdiction; their objective was assimilation. It was difficult afterwards to pursue our studies in another school. When I got out of the residential school, I registered for a technical course in Quebec. Unfortunately, before leaving, I got a ticket. I couldn't pay the ticket and so I was at-risk of going to prison for one month. I didn't talk to my father about it. I quit school because I didn't want them to find me. The following spring, I got married. Then I started working on the railroads as an apprentice electrician. I performed quality labour. People from the ministry came and offered me to follow the technical course that I had previously meant to follow. My boss told me that it was a great opportunity. I was going to accept, but then I found out that the ministry was only covering one year out of the three years of the course. I therefore decided to follow an intensive course in engineering drawing. I was never able to find work in my field in Schefferville. They would hire me as a day labourer or a custodian but never as a drafter. I was subjected to discrimination. My brother who was a mechanic was subjected to the same type of treatment.

Then, I worked for the band council. The people from the ministry would tell us that we were unable to administer ourselves. I took control of the situation. One year later, I went to meet with them and I challenged them to find a single mistake. My work was well done but it still wasn't good enough for them. They made me doubt my abilities. In order to numb the pain, I drank. Since I was in charge of paying the bills, I started asking questions to people from the ministry and the band council. I wanted to receive detailed invoices. The employees from the ministry were billing us for services that we weren't receiving. For a year, I refused to pay. They threatened to cut off our running water. I told them "We survived for thousands of years without a water system. Do what you have to do." They were using our budgets to operate the neighbouring town. It was a difficult time and so I was drinking. I also worked for the city. I experienced the same situation in Schefferville; I couldn't get a promotion because I was an Innu. I didn't want to deprive anyone of anything. All I wanted was to climb the ranks like everyone else, to earn my salary and be recognized for my labour, because I was a good worker. Being faced with this injustice also led me to drinking. One day, I told my boss "To understand, spend a single day in the skin of an Innu. Maybe then you'll see what it's like and lose your mind at night, my friend".

Of course it hurts, but our people are still alive despite all of the years spent fighting against assimilation. It wasn't only the government that was causing us harm; some individuals also wanted the submission of the Innu people. I had enough of it all. I started drinking alcohol again and kept drinking for years. I lost everything: my wife, my children and my job. Then, I pulled myself together. I stopped drinking and started working again. I was miserable because I didn't like myself. Everything I was seeing around me was telling me that the government was right after all. Shortly before the town closed, they offered me a job in my field. I quickly understood why: the white people knew that the mine was closing and they were leaving as soon as they could. Since I wanted the work experience, I accepted. The engineer was always looking over my shoulder. I ended up telling him "Look somewhere else, you're interfering with my work." He simply couldn't believe that an Innu could do this work so well. They were so prejudiced. If we give up, we become what others want us to become.

In 1987, I went into the forest with my brother. I stayed there for three years. I had to learn everything I had forgotten because of the residential school all over again; I didn't know anything about the forest anymore. I had to re-examine my values and gain respect for the knowledge of the Elders. One day I was with my father. He was walking in front of me. I felt so proud and carefree; I finally felt like a complete person. In the forest, everything they said about me at the residential school just went away. Ever since that day, I know that their maliciousness came directly from their ignorance. That was the problem. Today I know what I'm worth.

When I left the forest, I decided to undergo therapy. This time, I didn't let anyone choose for me. I opted for what was good for me instead of what was imposed upon me. I had already been down that road and I knew that it didn't lead anywhere. I am a member of a courageous people with a wealth of knowledge and great spirituality. For a time, we set our values aside. I don't have a lot of knowledge but I know where I come from. What I lost along the way, I'm going to try to get it back. Unfortunately, it will not be possible to integrate all of my father's knowledge. So I turned towards the values of my ancestors. When we really want something, we can succeed. The important thing is to respect yourself and do things on your own without expecting anything from others. Some people were unable to recover their identity and now their children are paying the price for it.

The government must cease imposing its authority upon us and return to the Aboriginal people of Canada their dignity. Through the power of money, they are keeping us dependent. They know how vulnerable we are. Our people can rise again; there is a lot of potential in our communities. I believe that or else I wouldn't be here. Everyone must make an effort. The youth must get an education. Without education, the money with kill us. We will be unable to deal with change. The other day, I met three Innu nurses. I was proud of them and I told them so. They are role models for our youth. That is how our people will rise up once again.

There is still an assimilation policy in place but it is less visible. Our schools must have maps that include Innu names and the outlines of the territories of our parents. The youth know where they come from. It's important for them to remember the past.

By the time we notice the damages caused to the environment it is often too late. Sometimes I ask myself "Am I the only one who sees that something is wrong?" We often talk about global warming or people's negligence with respect to the earth. I believe that we can turn it around. Our people see the changes. We see birds that never came here before. The animals are as confused as we are.

"During the ceremony, I heard the voices of our grandfathers, our great-grandfathers and our ancestors. The others couldn't hear them; I could hear them. They were saying that they were there to protect us. There were many of them in the tent."

Fleur, "Uapukun", from the Innu Nation
Maliotenam residential school

I was seven or eight years old when my mother brought me to the residential school. I had yet to learn anything about our culture. We lived in Maliotenam and my father had found work in Schefferville. I had several brothers and sisters; we were eight children. Everything was going well for us at home. The first school I went to was the residential school. Some of my siblings were already at the residential school by the time I got there. I could see them and talk to them. My brothers would bring me to the skating rink. My sisters were with the older children.

Sometimes I was afraid. Fortunately, there was an older girl who took care of us; she protected us and supported us. One day, I remember well, I had lice and sores all over my head. It was in the month of December and my mother had come to visit us. She was very angry; she said that they were providing us with very poor care. In January, she refused to let me return to the residential school. My parents had moved to Shefferville by then since the mine had opened. My mother got rid of my lice and healed my sores; it was a long and difficult process. I didn't return to the residential school for several years. I had attended for approximately six months. Then, in the early 1960s, I went to school in Schefferville. There were two schools there: a Naskapi school and a white school. We were all together and we shared some pleasant times. At fourteen years of age, I returned to the residential school. I stayed there for two years.

My fondest memory of the residential school is a picnic that was organized to celebrate the end of the school year. Afterwards, I spent the summer with my family. At seventeen years of age, I lacked discipline; I didn't follow the rules and so I was expelled. I would have preferred to have stayed because I had a lot of friends there. My brothers were there as well. In my case, the residential school was not a negative experience. I received a good education there.

Collection of life stories of the survivors of the Quebec Indian Residential Schools

Then, I was placed in foster families in Sept-Îles. It was more difficult than the residential school. I lived in Innu families. Today I still haven't forgiven those in charge of the residential school for having expelled me without ensuring my protection. My parents were not even informed that I was leaving the residential school. I was the one who told them at the end of the school year.

I was married for eighteen years. My husband also went to the residential school.

I got divorced when I stopped drinking. I made this decision for myself first and foremost, and then for my children as well. Alcohol was no longer providing me with any relief. I had friends who had succeeded in getting over their addictions issues with the help of therapy. I went to AA with them and I enjoyed it a lot.

My last therapy helped me a lot. This time, I did it for myself. Previously, I had undergone therapy to please my husband or my children. I went into the forest with a group. I really enjoyed the experience. I became aware of my weaknesses; I have problems with expressing my feelings and asserting myself. When I lived with my husband, he would always say to me "I don't want you to talk about me to others." I became a woman who didn't speak much; I was always afraid to talk.

I sometimes go to Sept-Îles; my sister lives there. I also have friends over there who work with women who are victims of violence. I feel free and relieved when I go to Schefferville for a while. I would like to follow another therapy in order to feel better and learn to assert myself more without worrying about what others think of me.

I work at the women's shelter. They ask me to talk to them about what happened at the residential school and I do it so that they understand our history. I tried to organize therapeutic sessions in the forest last year. My sister had accepted to lend us her cabin and we were going to bring our tents as well. We were supposed to leave in September but the project had to be cancelled because my ex-husband became ill. Now, I could start organizing it all over again. I would need someone to help me preside over the ceremony. It would be great if the Elders in the community could teach us how to preside over our ceremonies. I know an Elder who practices this ritual in the forest – in silence.

I am trying to reconnect with my spirituality and culture. I know that it will be good for me. I've gone into sweat lodges on two separate occasions. The first time, I wanted to see what it was all about. At first, I was afraid. We were many in the sweat lodge and it was very hot. I had to remove my glasses and my jewellery. A woman nearby said to me "Do not be afraid." She was the one who was holding the Talking Stick. A man from Saskatchewan had brought sacred items that he placed in the centre in order to share them with everyone. It made me proud to be a First Nations member. I was happy that he had come to share his sacred objects with the Innu people in order to enrich the memory of our past. During the ceremony, I heard the voices of our grandfathers, our great-grandfathers and our ancestors. The others couldn't hear them, but I could hear them. They were saying that they were there to protect us. There were many of them in the tent. I went outside to check if it was real or if it was a recording. It was real. When I talked to my friend about it, she believed me. Ever since that day, I have faith. Sometimes, I have premonitions. I know when an event or a death will occur. I can sense it, I can see it. I don't know why or how it comes to me. I take it as a message from our ancestors for the well-being of our community.

Photo: Patrice Gosselin

116

"From the starting point to the finishing point while following the cycle of the seasons, that is what I want to teach my son. I want to leave a path over the family lands and allow my children to participate in the return of each Anishnabe season. It is necessary to be patient, the wait is very long."

Noyeh

Pashkoshtegwan is my name according to Anishinabe tradition, it means *the one with no hair on his head*. I attended the Saint-Marc-de-Figuery residential school.

At the residential school, they changed my name: Noyeh became Noël. Up to the age of eighteen years, my name was Noël Michel. Therefore up to that age, my existence was illegal. The State had registered my name under Joseph Noé Michel. I prefer the name that my mother gave to me: Noyè. I gave myself my traditional name: Pashkoshtegwan.

I was born in Grand Lac Victoria. When the grey bus arrived, we didn't know what was happening to us. There was a crowd of people. We were told "Get dressed, get ready, we are taking you away. You are leaving." Sitting on the bus, I saw my grandmother disappear without knowing where I was going.

As soon as I stepped into the residential school, I felt like a hare caught in a snare. I remember once I went trapping with my aunt and she said to me, "If you find a hare that's still alive, remove the snare and bring it home. We'll keep it for two or three days and then we'll let it go." That's how I saw my first hare. He was stuck, but he hadn't moved. He had managed to survive for I don't know how long, so I removed the snare and brought him home. Two or three days later, we let him go.

That's how I felt at the residential school. I cried for an entire week. I couldn't deal with what was happening. I was lucky because a young boy my age from my community, a childhood friend, came to see me and he told me, "Don't worry, we'll get out of here one day, and then we'll return home." His words gave me courage and I told myself, "It's alright, one day we'll go back home." If it wasn't for him, I don't know how things would have turned out. His name is Charly. What he did for me, I did for others afterwards. The following year, I welcomed the new children too. Many were in the same state I was. I travelled the same path. It gave me courage and developed my sense of responsibility.

When I started going to the residential school, I believe I was seven years old. I was raised only by women until I was eleven years old: by my grandmother and then by the nuns. When I was ten years old, my grandmother passed away while I was still at the residential school. My grandmother was the one who always made sure I was picked up at the residential school and now she was gone. I didn't have the chance to attend her wake or her funeral.

When my grandmother passed away, I made the decision to take care of myself. When I left the residential school in the month of June as an eleven year old boy, I didn't want to live with my uncle. I had a little brother that I had never lived with. I knew that he was on the same bus as I was and that he would get off somewhere. And so I told myself that I'd get off at the same place as he did. That was the first decision I made.

I took responsibility for educating myself but without losing respect for the members of my family. When the bus stopped in Lac Simon, I was weary. I was nowhere and I had nowhere to go. I sat down with my little suitcase and I watched everyone get off the bus. Then I saw a woman approach that all the children ran to. I knew that she was my aunt Suzanne. My little brother pulled her off to the side and talked to her. Then, she came to see me and asked "Where are you going?" I replied that I didn't know and that I hadn't decided yet. She said to me "We're going to Grenet Lake, if you would like to come with us, we're leaving." I stood and said to her, "Aunt, I will follow you but on one condition: tomorrow I'm going to work." I was only eleven years old.

At Lake Grenet, she said to me "My two sons-in-law are there, if you want to work, I will speak to them for you." She went and spoke with Henry. He came to see me and said to me, "You want to work? You're starting tomorrow morning at five o'clock."

The following morning, I followed him. It was my first job. On large steel boats, we gathered eight-foot logs near the shores. For three years, I was a logger thanks to Henry who taught me the trade. I had the opportunity to take my destiny in my own hands and improve my situation. And that's what I did.

At the residential school, I was subjected to violence. I managed to get through it thanks to this voice that kept telling me, "It will all pass." By repeating that to myself, it gave me courage but, at the same time, it made the things I was going through seem "normal". Over the years, it was as if I was shutting my eyes and saying, "Alright then, I'll just take it." It was as if I had accepted being treated in this way, I was normalizing the situation. Despite everything, I learned many things and received a good education. At all levels, I was an average student and able to get by.

One of the nice things I experienced happened outside of the residential school. It was when I was selected as the artist of the year. I had a Quebecker friend whose father had a show room. All of the bands back then such as the Sultans, the Baronets and the Classels played there. I had obtained a ticket because I served as a custodian. My friend and I decorated the room. Every night, people said that the place looked nice. It made me happy. At the residential school the nuns and priests would never say to us, "You're good" or "You've got talent". They would never say such things.

Later in Amos, when I was in grade nine, the principal announced that our class would be organizing the graduation ceremony for the grade eleven class. My friend said to me, "Now's your chance to show everyone your talent." It was a large room and I completely decorated it – it took me the entire day. It was the hippy period, the flower power era, and so that's what I focused on. When the students arrived for their graduation, they were stupefied. I was shy. When the show was over, they called out my name and asked me to show myself before the crowd. It was a rare occurrence for an Indian to receive accolades in a white school. There were approximately five or six Indians in that school. I felt satisfaction; I knew that I had made my mark and I also knew that I eventually wanted to work in that field - in the artistic domain.

Then, I started doing the same types of things others did – I began drinking alcohol and using drugs. I liked it when people saw me and told me that I was cool. I was afraid of the normal people.

At eighteen years of age, I dreamed of having a son. Today he is sixteen years old. I also have three other children, my daughter-in-law's children. I adopted one of them. I rebuilt my family – it's my pride and joy.

I did a lot of searching to find a balance with respect to my spirituality, my health, my emotions and my physical appearance. At one point, I didn't believe in anything anymore, I was perturbed and uncomfortable with that. Eventually, I asked myself, "What does it mean to be an Anishnabe?" What does it mean to be a traditional Anishnabe or a purely traditional one? Ideally, one must establish a connection with the urban setting. It is important to find that balance. I succeeded in forging my identity through arts and music. For the past ten years, I've been speaking and singing. To you, I may be an unknown artist, but here, I am well known. We sing in our language, we exist in our language. That's a result of my Anishnabe soul, that's what establishes my balance.

My most important balance is the one I created with my children. I lived my youth in the hippy, disco, rock and new wave era. As an artist, I identify myself as an Anishnabe. When someone calls me an Indian, I tell them, "No, I'm an Anishnabe." The First Nations from around here call us the "bark eaters". We are not Algonquins, we are the Anishnabe.

Today, despite the impacts of the residential school, I believe that it's up to me now to take control of my life and say to myself, "These are my roots, this is my name, this is what I am, and this is who I am." That is my strength now. When I meet people, I tell them to try to find their balance like we have found our balance between the two cultures and two types of music, between traditional singing, drums and hip hop. That is the message I give to young musicians: "Learn from both worlds to create your own world but please, be Anishnabe."

My friend Charly and I shared the residential school experience until life separated us. He gave me words of courage. I am always grateful to those who have helped me. Our parents didn't say to us, "I love you." To my son who is sixteen years old today, I tell him every day. I tell my other children as well. That's what I missed. One of my children is part Haitian and part from our land, one is part African and part from our land and another is purely Anishnabe.

The only genuine heritage that we received from our parents is the territory – our traditional lands. I often tell my son that according to patriarchal tradition, I am the family elder and the chief of a land. After me, it will be his turn. He will have to carry on for me and assume the associated responsibilities. That's the tradition. The reason why I wanted to adopt another boy was because I wanted to create another branch in my family tree. I gave him my name as well as traditional land. He will have a home. I want to leave my child with a heritage. Here in the reserve, we cannot own anything. I built a house on my parents' land to leave to my children. Before, I didn't understand the importance of being the elder and having traditional land. From the starting point to the finishing point while following the cycle of the seasons, that is what I want to teach my son. I want to leave a path over the family lands and allow my children to participate in the return of each Anishinabe season. It is necessary to be patient, the wait is very long.

Statement of Apology – to former students of Indian Residential Schools

The treatment of children in Indian Residential Schools is a sad chapter in our history.

For more than a century, Indian Residential Schools separated over 150,000 Aboriginal children from their families and communities. In the 1870s, the federal government, partly in order to meet its obligation to educate Aboriginal children, began to play a role in the development and administration of these schools. Two primary objectives of the Residential Schools system were to remove and isolate children from the influence of their homes, families, traditions and cultures, and to assimilate them into the dominant culture. These objectives were based on the assumption Aboriginal cultures and spiritual beliefs were inferior and unequal. Indeed, some sought, as it was infamously said, "to kill the Indian in the child". Today, we recognize that this policy of assimilation was wrong, has caused great harm, and has no place in our country.

One hundred and thirty-two federally-supported schools were located in every province and territory, except Newfoundland, New Brunswick and Prince Edward Island. Most schools were operated as "joint ventures" with Anglican, Catholic, Presbyterian or United Churches. The Government of Canada built an educational system in which very young children were often forcibly removed from their homes, often taken far from their communities. Many were inadequately fed, clothed and housed. All were deprived of the care and nurturing of their parents, grandparents and communities.

First Nations, Inuit and Métis languages and cultural practices were prohibited in these schools. Tragically, some of these children died while attending residential schools and others never returned home.

The government now recognizes that the consequences of the Indian Residential Schools policy were profoundly negative and that this policy has had a lasting and damaging impact on Aboriginal culture, heritage and language. While some former students have spoken positively about their experiences at residential schools, these stories are far overshadowed by tragic accounts of the emotional, physical and sexual abuse and neglect of helpless children, and their separation from powerless families and communities.

The legacy of Indian Residential Schools has contributed to social problems that continue to exist in many communities today.

It has taken extraordinary courage for the thousands of survivors that have come forward to speak publicly about the abuse they suffered. It is a testament to their resilience as individuals and to the strength of their cultures. Regrettably, many former students are not with us today and died never having received a full apology from the Government of Canada.

June 11, 2008

The government recognizes that the absence of an apology has been an impediment to healing and reconciliation. Therefore, on behalf of the Government of Canada and all Canadians, I stand before you, in this Chamber so central to our life as a country, to apologize to Aboriginal peoples for Canada's role in the Indian Residential Schools system.

To the approximately 80,000 living former students, and all family members and communities, the Government of Canada now recognizes that it was wrong to forcibly remove children from their homes and we apologize for having done this. We now recognize that it was wrong to separate children from rich and vibrant cultures and traditions, that it created a void in many lives and communities, and we apologize for having done this. We now recognize that, in separating children from their families, we undermined the ability of many to adequately parent their own children and sowed the seeds for generations to follow, and we apologize for having done this. We now recognize that, far too often, these institutions gave rise to abuse or neglect and were inadequately controlled, and we apologize for failing to protect you. Not only did you suffer these abuses as children, but as you became parents, you were powerless to protect your own children from suffering the same experience, and for this we are sorry.

The burden of this experience has been on your shoulders for far too long. The burden is properly ours as a Government, and as a country. There is no place in Canada for the attitudes that inspired the Indian Residential Schools system to ever again prevail. You have been working on recovering from this experience for a long time and in a very real sense, we are now joining you on this journey.

The Government of Canada sincerely apologizes and asks the forgiveness of the Aboriginal peoples of this country for failing them so profoundly.

In moving towards healing, reconciliation and resolution of the sad legacy of Indian Residential Schools, implementation of the Indian Residential Schools Settlement Agreement began on September 19, 2007. Years of work by survivors, communities, and Aboriginal organizations culminated in an agreement that gives us a new beginning and an opportunity to move forward together in partnership. A cornerstone of the Settlement Agreement is the Indian Residential Schools Truth and Reconciliation Commission. This Commission presents a unique opportunity to educate all Canadians on the Indian Residential Schools system. It will be a positive step in forging a new relationship between Aboriginal peoples and other Canadians, a relationship based on the knowledge of our shared history, a respect for each other and a desire to move forward together with a renewed understanding that strong families, strong communities and vibrant cultures and traditions will contribute to a stronger Canada for all of us.

On behalf of the Government of Canada
The Right Honourable Stephen Harper,
Prime Minister of Canada

Reflection

Reflection

Reflection

Reflection

Reflection